P9-DDX-272

THE LEADERSHIP LIBRARY
VOLUME 12
LEADERS

Other books in THE LEADERSHIP LIBRARY

Well-Intentioned Dragons by Marshall Shelley

Liberating the Leader's Prayer Life by Terry Muck

Clergy Couples in Crisis by Dean Merrill

When It's Time to Move by Paul D. Robbins, ed.

Learning to Lead by Fred Smith

What Every Pastor Needs to Know about Music, Youth, and Education
   by Garth Bolinder, Tom McKee, and John Cionca

Helping Those Who Don't Want Help by Marshall Shelley

Preaching to Convince by James D. Berkley, ed.

When to Take a Risk by Terry Muck

Weddings, Funerals, and Special Events
   by Eugene Peterson, Calvin Miller, and others

Making the Most of Mistakes by James D. Berkley

THE LEADERSHIP LIBRARY

Volume

12 | Leaders

Learning Leadership from Some of Christianity's Best

Harold Myra, ed.

Carol Stream, Illinois

WORD BOOKS
PUBLISHER
WACO, TEXAS

WORD, CANADA
RICHMOND, B.C.

LEADERS

©1987 Christianity Today, Inc.

A LEADERSHIP/Word Book. Copublished by Christianity Today, Inc. and Word, Inc. Distributed by Word Books.

Cover art by Joe Van Severen

Library of Congress Cataloging-in-Publication Data

Leaders.

LEADERS: Learning leadership from some of Christianity's best / Harold Myra, ed.
    p.   c.m — (The Leadership library ; v. 12)
      "A Leadership/Word book."
      ISBN 0-917463-16-1 :
      1. Christian leadership.   2. Clergy—Office.   3. Pastoral
    theology.   I. Myra, Harold Lawrence, 1939- . II. Series.
BV652.1.L39 1987   87-18465
253—dc19   CIP

Printed in the United States of America

CONTENTS

76385

INTRODUCTION

Some must follow, and some command,
though all are made of clay.

LONGFELLOW

Leadership is a puzzling, paradoxical art. It demands both broad vision and attention to detail. It simultaneously calls for uncanny intuition and hard-headed analysis. It means often standing alone, yet proves itself in its ability to rally people. Leading isn't easy.

Leading a church holds particular challenges. Fred Smith confesses, "One morning I thought, 'What if today I were a pastor instead of a corporation president?' That idea scared me to death."

Thus *Leaders*. This book is for those pastors who sense the call to leadership but realize it is a high calling indeed. It's for those who are good leaders and would like to become great leaders.

Fortune 500 companies spend millions annually teaching employees to motivate, organize, communicate, and put out fires. In the process, business has tapped an ancient secret: mentors. People learn to lead by spending time with people of proven leadership ability, by talking to them and sifting their responses. Middle managers are paired with senior executives, and through that interaction, begin to assimilate the qualities that make for strong leaders.

That's the dynamic of *Leaders*.

From people who've taken charge, you'll hear no-nonsense replies to questions like these:

What are the leader's priorities? And how do you set and maintain them?

How do you deal with criticism?

How do you handle conflict within the group?

What's the best way to initiate change?

How do you motivate people to do their best?

Consistent with the vision of THE LEADERSHIP LIBRARY, *Leaders* offers not ivory-tower ideas that ought to work, but front-lines ideas that *have* worked — from people who make things happen in business, government, higher education, and the church. Harold Myra, president and CEO of Christianity Today, Inc., has tied together the thirteen varied interviews (some previously published in LEADERSHIP, some not) with a chapter describing his own hard-won insights into leadership.

We think you'll enjoy sitting and talking with the leaders in these pages. You may nod your head at some of the things they say, and shake it at others. But we believe you'll be enriched through your time with these Christians who have demonstrated the ability to lead.

It's our privilege to introduce them to you.

— Kevin Miller
Associate Editor, LEADERSHIP

The books in THE LEADERSHIP LIBRARY are generally team efforts, and this one is especially so. I'm grateful not only to the people who agreed to be interviewed for LEADERSHIP and this volume, but the many who conducted the interviews: Terry Muck, Paul Robbins, Dean Merrill, Marshall Shelley, Jim Berkley, Dan Pawley, and Donald Bubna. Kevin Miller did the lion's share of the hands-on editing, and Bonnie Rice handled a variety of projects with characteristic aplomb.

— Harold Myra

ONE

LEADERSHIP: A UNIQUE, PERSONAL MOSAIC

We must learn common leadership principles, but power is released as we become true to our God-given personalities.

HAROLD MYRA

E very leader is unique — magnificently unique. We humans made in God's image are each a distinct universe, and though there may be general principles of leadership we can apply, we all must develop our individual, personal mosaics.

The leaders interviewed in this book are in some ways studies in contrasts. I think back to our discussions in a suburban living room with Fred Smith for LEADERSHIP's first interview. The memory of his darting wit contrasts with, say, that of Richard Halverson's open earnestness in an O'Hare Airport room . . . or Howard Hendricks's lively but professorial interaction in a Dallas coffee shop . . . or Eugene Peterson's low-key yet penetrating blend of pastoral insight and literary allusion in CTi's conference room.

I looked up the introduction for that first LEADERSHIP interview and found this description of Fred: "He possesses not only the fastest but the most fitting quip for every occasion. His humor is always sneaking up on you from the most unlikely angles. But Fred's is never surface humor — it's lightning-crisp communication. He answers questions with stories and elliptical insights that blow open preconceived ideas. Fred often speaks on two or three levels of humor at the same time, and you have to be watching his eyes for the twinkle and his face for the precise expression to punctuate his meaning."

Fred is unique, and humor and depth of insight are only part of his individuality. Each of the leaders interviewed in this book showed commonalities such as intense commitment to Christ and deep ministry insights. But there's a rich diversity in their personalities; they have played to their strengths and flourished as individuals.

The task is to learn from them without becoming mimics. How can we develop, as they have, our unique personalities in response to God's call?

Observing the human response to leadership needs, I'm increasingly convinced diversity is the way God runs not only his universe but his church. God didn't make giraffes at all like hummingbirds, except they both eat, breathe, and beautifully glorify him. Ocelots and beavers, hawks and ptarmigans — what amazing diversity in God's creation! In the same sense, this brilliantly creative Creator has made personalities, and therefore leadership styles, as diverse as giraffes and hummingbirds. We must learn common principles, but a certain power is released as we become true to our God-given personalities.

Recently in a phone conversation, Fred mentioned he was reading a book titled *What Works for Me,* written by a number of top corporate executives. Fred described the book with some enthusiasm, but what appealed to me most was the title itself. It didn't promise too much. It simply said, "This approach works for me; maybe it will work for you."

Here is the spirit with which one might read this book, and any similar one. Every insight and concept should be sifted through a personal, scripturally informed screen.

Over the years, a number of principles have emerged for me as I've attempted to sift concepts. Those that follow are nuggets that have helped me in creating a personal mosaic — one that balances individuality and God's sovereignty.

The Beginning Point Is Obvious

How trite to say that it all starts with prayer. Yet how thoroughly true. Again and again in our leadership we come to the point of realizing how fully helpless we are. Jesus said he could do "nothing without the Father," yet we so frequently forget we are surely no more powerful than he!

As you read the interview with Henri Nouwen and Richard Foster, I hope you catch some of the power there. After the hours of dialogue you see boiled down to print, I drove home, full of a sense of prayer at work. I walked the streets near my home for two hours, lifted in an unusual way, joyous with the certainty that God was in charge of this world, despite the Gulag and Beirut, despite children molested, women humiliated, fathers imprisoned.

I frequently do not feel that way. It is only through prayer that life on this planet begins to make any sense at all. The truth is, we are going to change things relatively little; the necessity is to "see through God's glasses." Only then can we possibly begin to give genuinely Christian leadership.

Prayer becomes the center. Luther tells us that as it is the business of cobblers to make shoes, so it's our business as Christians to pray. This sort of statement, our surveys in LEADERSHIP Journal tell us, causes considerable guilt among Christian leaders. Yet it is in actuality an affirmation of a powerful priority that puts all else in perspective and makes genuinely spiritual work possible. Work without prayer is a terrible danger. In fact, our Christian work can quickly become an enemy.

About twenty years ago I read the statement, "A man with a burning purpose draws others to himself, who help him to fulfill it." That had a powerful effect on me; it penetrated to the heart of my perception of my task and future and helped me become effective. Yet I also sensed how utterly critical it was that the burning purpose be centered in prayer, for such intensity can become the Devil's furnace. Despite our constant belief to the contrary, no words are more ultimately true than, "Without me, ye can do nothing."

Leaders Must Be Realists

Our perception of the Christian life often draws on the scriptural analogies of seeds and harvest, and visions of well-ordered gardens with rows of well-pruned trees heavy with fruit. However, the scene that bursts into my mind is that of a sprawling, sweaty, unpredictable ranch. It's full of life all right, but not at all well ordered. Calves bawl in terror, a jackass kicks the milk pail into the manure, and a teenager laments it's his turn to clean out the barn. Bloody birth and bitter death and the exuberant kicks and leaps of a newborn foal all combine to make life bittersweet.

Ehud's dagger in a fat belly and King Saul's selfishness typify the realism of Scripture. Last week I stood in the kitchen of a retreat center talking to a young woman dramatically impacted by the failures of leaders. The president of the Christian college she had attended and who had spoken so eloquently of following Christ had deserted his wife for another woman. In addition, the college dean, her spiritual mentor, also got a divorce. Subsequent events in her own family were equally devastating.

As we talked in the kitchen, we agreed life is a great deal more tragic than we are led to expect in Sunday school. It is not only more tragic in the sense of leukemia, hurricanes, and auto crashes. It is tragic in the sense of people struggling to follow Christ and do right but ending up making terrible botches of their lives.

For instance, how many leaders have experienced betrayal, not from hostile enemies but from those who have labored beside them, often in top positions in the church? Not that great numbers of fellow Christians are Judases, but our egos and radically different perceptions and agendas make such wrenching experiences seem nearly inevitable. Our surveys included in the Winter 1981 LEADERSHIP article on betrayal convinced me "righteous people" are frequently dumbfounded at the actions of equally righteous individuals who see it differently. More than half of those surveyed had experienced "traumatic events extemely difficult to accept."

The leader is an earthy farmer. Whether the analogy is putting manure around roots or pouring medicine down a cow's throat, leaders must expect many nasty moments and unpleasant surprises.

Applicable Truths Lurk Everywhere

Leaders must aggressively seek out adaptable insights. In reading the pages of this book, we should not be dismayed if the settings and approaches at times seem alien to our situations. Applicable truths are often found in settings totally different from our own.

I was disturbed to read a study that indicated the vast majority of people simply cannot transfer principles from one discipline to another. Most people need someone else to point out how, say, a sociologist's book on Eskimos might apply to teaching math. In the study, researchers found most people in one discipline could apply data and concepts only within their own fields. They could not take the needed creative leaps from one field to another. No wonder we need an army of instructors in colleges and seminaries ladling out specialty packages of general truths!

In reality, the creative process presents all the world as a vast picking ground for applicable truth. It should be thoroughly natural to apply a principle found, say, in a *Fortune* magazine article on chicken farming to, perhaps, sermon preparation (no humor intended!). What the study suggests to me is that the few who can make these constant and creative transfers and applications from disparate sources — literature, sports, travel, leisure, whatever — are the few who can conceptualize and adapt and therefore lead within their unique settings. Shaping our personal mosaics involves transfer and integration from a vast variety of sources.

Sorting Starts with Gratitude for Ourselves

Because of the nearly infinite number of sources, the only way one might even begin to choose and integrate insights is marked by what may seem an odd starting point. It is this: First, we must accept ourselves. Without the grid of our own personalities and gifts as a basis with which to work, how can we begin the process of sorting?

The simple maxim of accepting ourselves is oft repeated, but just as frequently denied. Again and again we hear speakers say they feel writers are the persons with deeper, more lasting worth. Writers are intimidated by speakers, administrators wish they could sing, and soloists feel like manipulated commodities. It may be trite to say we must all be parts of an orchestra. Yet this vision often told to children eludes most adults.

Effective leadership calls for glorying in our distinct contributions, whatever their nature or limitations.

I was startled one day by a casual observation made by Billy Graham. He said he felt his "real gift" was writing his fundraising letters. The statement caught me off guard. What did he mean? He wasn't denigrating his preaching, although it's well known that he refers to himself as a simple gospel preacher. He was simply sensing the importance of a personal gift easily undervalued. He cares deeply about those letters that carry his name and share his heart and concerns with his supporters. That's a vital part of his leadership, as is his voluminous personal correspondence, which may often feel to him like a mundane burden.

We all get involved with menial functions, correspondence among them. Yet the sense of God's call and the drama of our gifts being used can give even correspondence and tedious desk work a value that goes beyond our feelings and perceptions.

Again, we must be realists. Yesterday I talked for some time with a CTi editor about the tension between all the bland things that must be done year after year and the tasks and opportunities that stretch us. Most of us face mountains of work that gets the job done but makes us, if not bored, somewhat dissatisfied. Our strongest gifts are no guarantee that God will use them. Today, there is a great deal of emphasis on finding our gifts and using them. Well and good. At CTi we work very, very hard to get people into just the right "harnesses." Yet in a broken world, many gifts will go unused, and for the Christian, God's direct leadership frequently overrules our logic.

I've been impressed by the example of Oswald Chambers, who has greatly enriched my life with spiritual insights. As a young man, he believed his gifts would be directed toward the arts. He wrote in 1895, "My lifework as I see it, my eternal work, is, in the almighty strength of God, to strike for the redemption of the aesthetic kingdom of the soul of man — music and art and poetry, or rather, the proving of Christ's redemption of it. . . . An ambition, a longing, has seized me, seized me so powerfully that it has convinced me of the need. The Spirit of God seems to cry, 'Whom shall I send, and who will go for us?' "

Despite this conviction that not only his gifts but his call lay in the arts, subsequent events indicated otherwise. He kept stifling the idea of entering the ministry. Yet his art goals were constantly thwarted, and eventually, his determination to follow Christ led him to say this: "Brighter, clearer, and more exquisite is the spiritual within becoming, and my whole being is ablaze and passionately on fire to preach Christ. It is the almighty love of God that constrains me, and in the midst of a keen consciousness of a complete unworthiness, my soul cries out within me, 'Here am I, send me.' " How delightfully ironic, in the sovereignty of God, that Chambers's poetic and artistic abilities shine like rubies and sapphires in his recorded sermons and books, which have enriched the Christian world.

C. S. Lewis comments that "the lion must roar," and we need to be true to our deepest creative drives whenever possible. But a mysterious alchemy is at work between God, man, and environment.

Fill the Box!

Joe Bayly for many years was fond of challenging people with the fact that all of us find ourselves in a box. It may be a big box or a small one. It may have an odd shape or be reasonably symmetrical. But we all find ourselves in a box of limitations and opportunities. Our task is not to bemoan the limitations or strut because of the size of the box. If we've committed ourselves to the situation, we try to understand the box and fill it — every corner and cranny — with all the creativity and energy possible.

As we fill the box, we may find it expanding to make room for the new realities. Or we may find ourselves moving on to a different box (not necessarily a larger one). Or we may find the box changing shapes in fascinating, enriching, perhaps discouraging ways. Whatever the changes, every human being is in a series of boxes, many of them bordering on the outrageous, all through life. We are called to understand the limitations but press them for all they're worth.

A decade ago I found myself in a Washington, D.C. coffee shop early in the morning eating a sweet roll and asking myself, *What in the world am I doing here?* The job I had just taken with *Christianity Today* was full of ridiculous situations that seemed not only unresolvable but downright silly. The tacky coffee shop seemed to reflect precisely the box I found myself in.

Yet as I sat drinking coffee and talking to the Lord, almost as if the words were written across the beige wall in front of me, this phrase struck home: "For this cause were ye brought to the kingdom." The verse may have been out of context, but it struck in me like a clapper striking a bell. No matter how absurd, tacky, or infuriating, this was precisely what I had been prepared for, precisely the battle to be waged. The phrase lifted me into that day and to the commitments ahead.

"For this cause were ye brought to the kingdom." Time and again at *Christianity Today*, when my emotions said the circumstances were beneath contempt, unworthy of my energies — when the vocabulary the Marine Corps once acquainted me with seemed most appropriate — that phrase has jolted me back to the sense of purpose within limitations. This cause. This moment. This box, no matter how discouraging, or perhaps humiliating.

An Effective Sorting Process

So we accept ourselves and we accept the sometimes brutal, sometimes banal realities of life as we search for adaptable information through a scriptural grid. We keep a sense of expectancy that clues will appear as we use a tough-minded sorting process. Since leadership requires a large volume and high quality of information wisely applied, we use a great variety of sources.

It helps me to think of oranges, waves and waves of oranges rolling into vast bins to be sorted. A certain size hole accepts only a certain size orange. Ideas and concepts come at us in high volume, and picking out the ones that apply to us and our situations can be an invigorating process.

This includes both rejecting and/or modifying good ideas and advice. For instance, after three years at my first job, I learned that my mentor and supervisor, Ron Wilson, had decided to leave for other challenges. I was to take on many of his responsibilities, so I asked him, "If there is one thing you would advise me to do, one word of counsel, what would it be?"

He thought a moment and replied, "I would travel. A journalist needs to get out and see what's going on. Broaden your understanding."

Not long after that I read a less enthusiastic assessment of travel in *The Effective Executive* by Peter Drucker: "Professor C. Northcote Parkinson has pointed out in one of his delightful satires that the quickest way to get rid of an inconvenient superior is to make a world traveler out of him. The jet plane is indeed overrated as a management tool. A great many trips have to be made; but a junior can make most of them."

As I recently reread *The Effective Executive*, that quote reverberated in me: "Aha! That's where I got that perception twenty years ago." I had sensed that my task was journalistic management and that for me, limited travel would work best. The point is not that Wilson was wrong and Drucker right. Both statements were valid. But my strengths and goals concerned being a catalyst, journalist, and manager.

Actually, limiting travel meant bucking the norm a bit among my jetting peers. One must, however, set his own course. I loved reading not long ago a startling fact about Ray Bradbury. One of the most recognized writers of science fiction, author of *The Martian Chronicles*, he has never gotten on an airplane! He says he never will, this man who has written so eloquently about riding in interplanetary rockets. Can you imagine how often people must accuse him of being parochial and insulated? Or give him a hundred legitimate and pressing reasons for a quick trip to the East Coast?

The fact he will not himself leave the earth for the "friendly skies" I find not only ironic but oddly comforting. The article I read gave no reasons for his not flying. I prefer to think of his stance as a perfect picture of someone majoring on what works for him — of stubbornly running the oranges through his own sort.

Another item from *The Effective Executive* that strongly influenced me was an anecdote related to pruning back every possible task that can be handed off to others. Drucker explained that "there is not much risk that an executive will cut back too much. We usually tend to overrate rather than underrate our importance and to conclude that far too many things can be done only by ourselves. Even very effective executives still do a great many unnecessary, unproductive things.

"But the best proof that the danger of overpruning is a bugaboo is the extraordinary effectiveness so often attained by severely ill or severely handicapped people.

"A good example was Harry Hopkins, President Roosevelt's confidential adviser in World War II. A dying, indeed almost a dead man for whom every step was a torment, he could only work a few hours every other day or so. This forced him to cut out everything but truly vital matters. He did not lose effectiveness thereby; on the contrary, he became, as Churchill called him once, 'Lord Heart of the Matter' and acomplished more than anyone else in wartime Washington."

I cannot count the number of times that illustration has come into my mind at critical moments. I determined to ruthlessly cut away whatever was not crucial to the task, asking myself repeatedly, *If I had two hours per day or ten hours per week to do this job, what specific things would I do and what would I not do?* As Drucker indicates in many places, no matter how much wise pruning one does, the information worker will always have much more to do than he can possibly get to. As much as possible must be delegated to others.

Why all this autobiographical material? Simply as one illustration of the process of sorting through input from many sources, some of which seem unrelated. For instance, when I was editing *Campus Life* Magazine, I read *A Business and Its Beliefs*, the story of IBM by Thomas Watson, Jr. What did that have to do with editing a youth magazine? I found its three basic principles for working with and serving people highly relevant. At the same time insights from sources as disparate as Dostoyevsky, Paul Tournier, and the *Reader's Digest* were equally important.

This past summer a group of Christian leaders met with Peter Drucker in Colorado. We "sat at his feet," sorting through the wisdom of this Renaissance man. To me, it was highly significant that when asked the many questions we had relating to the church and ministry, he would as often dip back to illustrations from medieval history or Japanese culture as use contemporary illustrations. His net was spread from pre-Christian cultures to his boyhood days in Vienna. He drew out principles from events and human activity like a man hooking swordfish and marlin from the sea.

At the Colorado meeting, Drucker talked about people being divided into readers and listeners, those who primarily get their information from the eye or the ear. Generally, each of us leans one way or the other. He described Eisenhower's effectiveness at reading reports and press queries during the war in Europe. Ike handled the press brilliantly, reviewing each question on paper ahead of time. However, when he became president and started answering questions from the floor without being able to literally see them, he was caught off guard and didn't respond as deftly. The press then portrayed him as much less brilliant.

Drucker indicated it would be wise to let people, especially those we work closest with, know whether we are primarily readers or listeners. I've found it very helpful to understand about myself that something on paper has a much greater impact on me than a verbal presentation.

Drucker obviously has developed his own personal effectiveness from this wide range of insights. With all he has accomplished and currently achieves (some have called him the most influential thinker of the century), we were astounded to learn that he has no secretary and he answers his own phone. This for a man who writes constantly for the nation's major publications, teaches in a university, and is a leading expert on Japanese art.

How might he have arrived at this concept? He somehow applied his broad scope of insight and made part of his personal mosaic not managing anyone, perfect in its simplicity for what he wishes to accomplish — perhaps like Ray Bradbury staying off those jets.

As you read the rest of the chapters in this book, you might remember the image of Peter Drucker hooking insights from every source, or your own hands running oranges through a very personal sorting bin, or Chambers finding his first notions of a call and a career only a first step. It is indeed a strange alchemy between God and man and environment, and each one of us called to any sort of leadership will find it full of enigmas, surprises, and enormous opportunity.

Part I
CHARACTER

T W O

THREE TRAITS OF A LEADER

If a leader demonstrates competency, genuine concern for others, and admirable character, people will say, "I like what that person is doing. I'm going to follow him."

J. RICHARD CHASE

J. Richard Chase

Leadership begins with one person — the leader. A thousand people may be led or a dozen management skills exercised, but ultimately the leadership equation may be reduced to a lone person, one individual whom people follow.

What is a leader like? What qualities set this person apart?

These questions of character occupy the first two interviews. The first is with J. Richard Chase, since 1982 president of Wheaton College in Wheaton, Illinois.

Dick was formerly president of Biola University in La Mirada, California. During his twelve-year tenure, enrollment grew from 1,800 to 3,100 students, and graduate offerings were expanded greatly through Talbot Theological Seminary and Rosemead School of Psychology. Dick has served on numerous boards, including those of Mission Aviation Fellowship, the Christian College Coalition, and the National Association of Independent Colleges and Universities.

David Hubbard, president of Fuller Theological Seminary, has described Dick as having "a blue-chip reputation. He is known as very solid, no-nonsense . . . cautious and prudent." It's appropriate that one who has developed such a reputation discuss three traits essential to a leader.

Some leaders are outgoing; some introverted. Some can talk their way out of any situation, while others perform their way out. So what traits of a great leader are nonnegotiable? What traits can a leader not afford to lose?

Since my educational background is primarily in classical rhetoric, I'll start with the old classical questions: What are the dimensions of a person who has the leadership ethos? What kind of person has the manner of life that causes other people to follow him?

I would answer those questions by identifying three broad categories: *competency*, personal *character*, and genuine *concern* for others. This threefold concept is primarily associated with Aristotle, but it is also biblical. It is virtually the outline Paul uses in 1 Corinthians 9, when he defends his own apostolic leadership. He starts by mentioning his competency, then moves to genuine concern for others, and finally closes with character.

Leaders make decisions and take action; and if their leadership demonstrates competency, genuine concern for others, and admirable character, people will say, "I like what that person is doing. I'm going to follow him."

Let's start with competency. In the church, pastors are expected to be competent at many things, but particularly preaching. Can the pastor who is not a very good preacher be a successful leader?

Sure. I have known thriving churches where the pastor has not been strong in the pulpit. But in cases like that, the pastor was competent in communicating a knowledge of the Scriptures in other ways. He might not have been overly articulate or able to put words together well on Sundays, but he was unusually effective in small Bible studies, midweek services, or in homes over a cup of coffee.

Often the pastor was competent in putting together a staff. I know one church where the Sunday school staff carried the major load of formal biblical instruction for the church. And what was beautiful was that the pastor in no way felt threatened by these staff members. He chose them. So even though he was not outstanding in the pulpit, his competency in working with staff, in administrating, and in demonstrating genuine concern for people, had made him a dynamic, successful leader. Above all, he modeled biblical qualities of character.

In the business world, the same thing is true. Some businesses have been built by people who make you say, "He's not a leader. But the staff he's put together is powerful. How did he do that?"

That kind of leader had competency in some less-obvious area that attracted the vice-presidents or whoever was needed to do the job.

As leaders give away various tasks to others, what tasks remain uniquely their own?

There are very few tasks on the Wheaton College campus that I can do as well as the people hired to do them. In virtually every instance, I'm not as good as they are at their task.

The one area where I have to gain expertise is grasping the "broad view" of where the institution is going. Somebody has to have overall leadership of basic operations. But that person, by virtue of his need to see the broad view — and to stimulate others to pursue the broad goals of the institution — forfeits the opportunity to outperform others in specific tasks.

How do you define character?

By *character,* I mean a leader must have the kind of personal qualities that would-be followers respect. That's true for non-Christian leaders as well as Christian leaders.

Certainly the Christian leader must have godly character. The biblical view of leadership focuses far more on the quality of being than on the quality of doing. The passages in Titus, Timothy, Peter, and so on, are almost always about what kind of person you are. What should a bishop *be?* What should an elder *be?* What should the young man *be?*

Peter Drucker, in one of his books, comments that "quality of character" doesn't make a leader, but the lack of it flaws the entire process. God knows there are certain qualities required of a person to be a Christian leader. Without them, a Christian leader becomes useless to God.

The tragedy in our society is we're far less interested in measuring leaders by the biblical qualities of character than nonbiblical ones like a macho image.

One of the biblical qualities is being a servant. What does it mean to be a "servant leader"?

A leader meets people's needs, and you're not going to build a healthy church by doing it yourself. A lesson I have had a hard time learning is that you can't run a college by yourself. You have to get others involved.

So the servant leader is someone who is not only *not upset* if others are doing their thing, he is *providing the platform* where they can. If people are saying, "Hey, that was a great lesson today by the Sunday school teacher," the pastor doesn't say, "Well, what about my sermon?" Instead, he says, "I'm sure glad that teacher is here, aren't you?"

I know a pastor who has a small church in a small community. He's never going to have a church with five thousand members. But it may be that with the kind of impact he's had on that community and on individuals, a hundred years from now he might be viewed by church historians as a leader who produced a generation of leaders.

Do you feel God has shaped you specifically for leadership?

Looking back, I do. I see a number of difficult things I wish I had not had to go through, and many times I thought I wouldn't make it, but as a leader I have drawn heavily on some of these very difficult situations.

Once I was involved in a family business and some very expensive lawsuits were brought against the business. I recall coming to the place where I realized I had the Lord and my loved ones and that had to be sufficient. It took a lot of money and some good attorneys to finally get me extricated from the situation. But that experience made me far more understanding of people who find themselves in difficult binds. Instead of saying, "Well, you shouldn't have been in that situation," or "We can't use you," I understand now how people can get trapped and the support they need to survive and prevail.

Can leaders be trained?
Yes, I think they can. Going on the assumption that everybody has charisma for somebody, they can enhance that charisma by becoming competent in certain areas.

I think of Dwight D. Eisenhower, who many believe was a mediocre line officer and whose career was going no place. He requested to go to Panama, I think, to work under a certain general. That general had a transforming impact on his life as an officer; he taught Eisenhower how to become a competent leader.

How do you find your niche, that area in which you can become competent?
You shouldn't listen to Charles Swindoll and say, "I'm going to be like him," if you don't have his abilities. Despite his dedication to extensive study and prayer, he has the ability to see the helpful things we often miss, and he can communicate truth in memorable ways. And you can't listen to a lecture by Carl Henry and say, "I'm going to be like him," unless you have his theoretical ability and mental tenacity to see through a problem.

You shouldn't pick a model and say, "He's interesting; he has a following; I want to be like him." You need to say, "God, what are my gifts? Help me to see what they are, and help me to develop them to the best of my ability." That may mean that you will have fewer followers than other leaders, but the followers you have will be the ones God wants you to have.

Do you see a difference between leadership and management?
A definition I've run into says, "You manage what's there." Leaders should be good managers in the sense that they ought to be looking for more creative ways to enhance what

they're already doing. But if you equate management with maintenance, then you've got a problem. As a leader, you need to be out front, breaking new ground, providing vision. Maintenance can push aside visionary leadership, and that's not good.

Pastors easily get into that situation: They preach every Sunday, teach the Bible on Wednesday, and do discipling on another day, until there's little time to capture a vision, a new challenge for their congregations to impact the world for Christ. Managing can become a leadership role as long as it challenges others to do more than attend and listen.

Vision involves long-term goals. How do you impart such goals when many followers expect short-term results?

That's a problem I'm constantly wrestling with. The catch word for our age is *now*. Because of that, people favor short-range goals. I spoke two or three years ago at a long-range planning session, and afterward a person said to me, "Why do you do long-range planning? We've done it, and we find that nothing holds; everything changes before the goal is reached."

A leader, however, is part salesperson. The leader needs to make long-term goals desirable, and provide short-range stepping stones to get there.

How many important decisions do you make in a year?

Not many. The most important are the few key ones concerning staff and long-range goals. There are three or four of those watershed decisions a year. These are decisions where it is tough to redirect the action once the course is set.

I also participate in hundreds of decisions for which people come to me for final approval.

What would you consider your chief weaknesses as a leader?

Having been in senior administration for over twenty years now, I've concentrated on catching the big picture and on articulating it to the public. Because I get intrigued with the big picture, I like to see how it's working out. So my greatest fault is that I meddle too much.

I try to do it wisely, but I don't always. For example, I will sit down with a faculty member and while we're talking I'll get excited and prematurely share my vision for a program. It may be I've talked in generalities with the vice-president, and he hasn't had a chance to get going on the activity. That makes him look bad. I can create havoc that way.

Another problem I have involves letters I receive. People write the president because they're concerned. But I can't respond to every single one, and I can't meet with every person with a problem. There are just not enough hours in the day. So some correspondence has to be delegated. I feel if there is a problem and someone has written me, that person deserves a personal answer. So I tend to get more involved than I should.

Do you enjoy leading?

That's a tough question. I enjoy studying and practicing leadership, but I dislike its loneliness. I dislike the fact that sometimes the processes that went into a decision cannot be made known. You have to appear ignorant or off-base because you will do more harm if you explain *why* than if you just keep your mouth closed and move ahead. A lot of pastors feel that pressure following decisions regarding personnel; they're seldom at liberty to disclose all the reasons behind their decisions.

I also dislike conflict and strife, yet that is part of leadership.

Basically, I want to be thoroughly equipped at whatever I do, I want to be genuinely concerned about my brother, and I want to be the kind of person the Lord wants me to be. If I do those things, I will be demonstrating leadership.

T H R E E

THE SPIRITUAL LEADER'S VITALITY

Even spiritual exercises and disciplines can be terribly hollow. The real center is hearing God's voice and obeying his Word.

RICHARD FOSTER

As we are involved in unceasing thinking, so we are called to unceasing prayer.

HENRI NOUWEN

Richard Foster

Henri Nouwen

T he crying need of the spiritual leader, someone once pointed out, is "a sense of the spiritual center." But how does a leader develop that sense? What roads lead to increased spiritual vitality?

Discussing those questions are two men who have ventured on the inner journey and written eloquently of their travels.

Richard Foster has been a Quaker pastor in California and Oregon. He taught at George Fox College and now teaches at Friends University in Wichita, Kansas. He has written Celebration of Discipline; Freedom of Simplicity; and Money, Sex & Power (all Harper & Row), books that call for increased commitment to live the Christian life. Yet it's obvious from Foster's quick laugh and soft eyes that for him Christian commitment doesn't mean something hard and austere, but something warm and loving.

Henri J. M. Nouwen is a Catholic priest and psychologist who has taught at Notre Dame and Yale Divinity School. He is now priest-in-residence at the L'Arche Community near Toronto. Among Nouwen's many books are The Genesee Diary and The Wounded Healer (Doubleday), which take a look at what it means to be a Christian and a minister in modern society. But Nouwen's prophetic words are tempered by an intense, electric concern for those around him. He's easy to love, and his quick, reasoned thinking invites acceptance.

In reading their books, one realizes Foster and Nouwen are saying many of the same things. Yet they are from widely divergent traditions and use different language to express their thoughts. In this dialogue of a few years ago, they talk freely about getting to know God.

Since the spiritual life is such a personal matter, perhaps we could start with where each of you find yourself now in your spiritual journey. What's happening in your spiritual life?

Henri Nouwen: Spiritually, I'm in one of the most difficult periods of my life. At times I've felt my spiritual direction to be clear-cut; right now, however, everything is uncertain.

When I came from Holland to the United States, I became a diocesan priest, a psychologist, and a fellow at the Menninger Clinic. I joined the faculty at Notre Dame, taught in Holland, and came back to teach at Yale Divinity School. People started to respond more and more to what I had to say, and that led to an increasing sense of "Yes, I must have something to say." I earned an additional doctorate in theology, so I have all the credentials affirmed by the church and academia. I should be happy.

But these past months I've come face to face with my own spiritual abyss. None of this success has made me a more saintly or holy person. Let me try to describe what I mean. Last semester I traveled all over the world. I spoke to large audiences. I've never been so praised by such varied groups, from Southern Baptist to Greek Orthodox, from young people to old people. All this created a sense of having arrived. Yet my inner life was precisely the opposite of that. More and more I felt that if God has anything to say, he doesn't need me. I found myself experiencing two extremes at the same time: high affirmation and great darkness.

In the midst of this situation, I spent several prayerful days with some new Christian friends whom I had met at one of my lectures. During that time, I came in touch with my own brokenness in a new way. Those days together brought many valuable lessons. One of the most beautiful was that my friends experienced themselves as representatives of God's love, and discovered in themselves the ability to care for someone they had expected to learn from, not teach.

Richard Foster: I've had a similar experience, Henri. Back in my earlier years of coming to God, I was very intense; you know, I'M GOING TO GET CLOSE TO GOD! During that period, I once spent three days fasting and praying. After doing so, I felt an urging to call a man I had confidence in for his spiritual guidance. He lived at quite a distance, but I called and asked him if he would come and pray for me. He came, and I was ready to place myself before him and let him minister to me. Instead, he sat down in front of me and started confessing his sins. I thought, *I'm supposed to do that to you.* After he finished and I had prayed forgiveness for him, he said, "Now, do you still want me to pray for you?" All of a sudden I realized his discernment. He knew I had thought of him as a spiritual giant who was going to come and set me right. Only then did he place his hands on me and pray for me.

What made you believe so intensely that you needed to find God?
Foster: Desperation. Not so much for me at first, but for people I saw who needed help. Later, I began to feel how very much I also needed God.

Although there is a deep hunger in church leaders to spend time in solitude seeking God, many would say, "It's impossible for me. I'm trapped by the demands of my ministry."
Nouwen: I'm like many pastors; I commit myself to projects and plans and then wonder how I can get them all done. This is true of the pastor, the teacher, the administrator. Indeed, it's true of our culture, which tells us, "Do as much as you can or you'll never make it." In that sense, pastors are part of the world. I've discovered I cannot fight the demons of busyness directly. I cannot continuously say no to this or no to that, unless there is something ten times more attractive to choose. Saying no to my lust, my greed, my needs, and the world's powers takes an enormous amount of energy.

The only hope is to find something so obviously real and attractive that I can devote all my energies to saying yes. One such thing I can say yes to is when I come in touch with the fact that I am loved. Once I have found that in my total brokenness I am still loved, I become free from the compulsion of doing successful things.

Foster: Let me tie into that with an experience from the first church I pastored. I had finished my doctorate and I was supposed to be an expert. I went to a tiny church in Southern California that would rank as a marginal failure on the ecclesiastical scoreboards. I went in there and worked and planned and organized, determined to turn this church around. But things got worse. Anger seemed to permeate everyone: the conservatives were mad at the liberals, the liberals were mad at the radicals, and the radicals were mad at everyone else. I hated to go to pastors' conferences because I didn't have any success stories to tell. I was working myself to death, but it seemed to do no good. Then I spent three days with my spiritual director. Toward the end of that time he said, "Dick, you have to decide whether you are going to be a minister of this church or a minister of Christ." That was a turning point. Until then I had allowed other people's — and my own — expectations to manipulate me.

It's fascinating that we have two opposite illutrations here: Richard in an early pastorate that really wasn't successful, and Henri in a life full of successes, but both of them falling short of God's desires.

Foster: Yes, and even spiritual exercises and disciplines can be terribly hollow. The real center is hearing God's voice and obeying his Word.

You both talk about receiving spiritual guidance from other people. Richard spoke of his spiritual director. That's a term some Protestants will be unfamiliar with. What is a spiritual director? What authority does he or she have?

Foster: Spiritual directorship is a Christian idea. It means having someone who can read my soul and give me guidance in my walk with Christ. Many churches call it discipleship.

Nouwen: The church itself is a spiritual director. It tries to connect your story with God's story. Just to be a true part of this community means you are being directed, you are being guided, you are being asked to make connections.

The Bible is a spiritual director. People must read Scripture as a word for themselves and ask where God speaks to them.

Finally, individual Christians are also spiritual directors. The use of an individual person in spiritual direction has as many forms and styles as there are people. A spiritual director is a Christian man or woman who practices the disciplines of the church and of the Bible, and to whom you are willing to be accountable for your life in God. That guidance can happen once a week, once a month, or once a year. It can happen for ten minutes or ten hours. In times of loneliness or crisis, that person prays for you.

How do you find such a person?

Foster: This is itself a great adventure in prayer. I ask God to bring me someone, and then I wait for the salvation of God to come. My first director was an older woman who worked nights in a large hospital. Six days a week at eight in the morning, the end of the night shift, we met together to learn about prayer and to share our experiences with God. We began to learn what it means to walk with Christ, and the experience was a wonderful one for both of us. But it began by asking God to give me someone who would travel the road with me.

Many pastors don't feel there's anyone they can turn to for this kind of help.

Nouwen: If you are seriously interested in the spiritual life, finding a spiritual director is no problem. Many are standing around waiting to be asked. However, sometimes we don't want to get rid of our loneliness. There is something in us that wants to do it by ourselves. I constantly see this in my own life. It is so beautiful to realize we don't have to be lonely if we really want to become open to the dependency of God's love and the love of our fellow men and women. It isn't an easy dependency. If you allow someone to love you, that love will take you to painful places. When Abram became Abraham, it didn't get easy for him. When Saul became Paul, it didn't get easy for him, or for Simon when he became Peter. But it is so true that if I want to break out of my loneliness, God will send me his angels. A spiritual director is not a great guru who has it all together; it's just someone who shares his or her sinful struggles, and by doing so, reveals that there is a Presence that is forgiving.

Foster: I began to learn this in a pastorate in Oregon. It wasn't too long before I realized I needed people to help me. So in a dozen different ways I said, "Folks, I love you, and I need your help. I would love it if you would come to my office not just when you have a problem or when you are angry. Come any time and give me a booster shot of prayer." People began to stop by for ten minutes or so and pray for me. Grinning, they would say, "I've come to give you a booster shot of prayer." I'd get on my knees before these people in an act of submission and let them pray for me. It did wonderful things for my spirit.

Nouwen: Richard, I like the idea of asking people to come pray for you, but for some congregations that might be a little bit too explicit or formal. The very first thing for me to communicate to people is that I would really love to know them. In other words, I say, "Listen, come and tell me what is happening. Drop in. Interrupt. Constantly get me off my horse and throw me down and talk to me." The minister should be continuously interrupted. I'm always running somewhere, and I need people to say, "Stop! You didn't notice I was trying to say something to you."

How do you cope with those interruptions? Don't they derail you as well as help you?

Nouwen: What I'm talking about is having a spiritual attitude that wants to be surprised by God. We crowd our thoughts with so many agenda items that we don't take time to listen to God. God doesn't talk to me just at the end or at the beginning of a project but all the time; he may have me change directions in the middle. Now, I don't mean that you sit around waiting until God speaks in a burning bush. That may happen, but God also uses people to speak to you. Listen to them; stretch out your hand and let your people guide you.

The minister in one sense is a useless person; useless in that he or she can be used at any time by anyone for any thing. I was talking yesterday to a priest in Philadelphia who said, "I'm so worried about the summer; I'm a white priest in a black neighborhood. What do I do?" I replied, "Be sure to walk the streets. Make it clear that you are there. You don't have to talk all the time; just hang around. Tell the people you don't want anything. Act totally useless, waiting to be with them and love them."

What should happen at a spiritual retreat?
Nouwen: Prayer.
Foster: A silent period spent listening to God is indispensable. We often hear the question "How can busy pastors find time for a regular devotional life?" That's like asking, "How can auto mechanics find time to work on an automobile?"

It would be easy for a pastor reading this to feel enormous guilt. Some of the psychological studies indicate pastors may have insecure personalities, and that's one of the reasons they have gone into the pastorate. Yet they're susceptible to the pressures of pastoring. How can we help them get up in the morning and not run out simply to do the pressing and the urgent?
Foster: I was told in seminary that ideally if I preached from the Old Testament I should study the Hebrew text, and if I preached from the New Testament I should study the Greek text. I was told to spend time each week working on my sermon delivery. Pastoral counseling, they told me, is crucial to my ministry. I added up the time it takes to do all these things, and the total was staggering. And once in the ministry, I found out very quickly that those things might build churches, but they don't necessarily help people. So I had to go back to square one and ask, "What am I to do?" The answer that came was "Love God and walk with him." Once I am settled and centered on that, the guilt feelings aren't there about what I have to do or what I haven't done.

Nouwen: One of the most beautiful ways for spiritual formation to take place is to let your insecurity lead you closer to the Lord. Natural hypersensitivity can become an asset; it makes you aware of your need to be with people and it allows you to be more willing to look at their needs. In a sense, you let your psychological trembling become trembling for the Lord, and you use the insecurity of human relationships to develop a firm relationship with God.

Foster: The disciples are some of the best examples of that.

Nouwen: Your insecurity can be neurotic, but it can also lead to a deep spiritual life. Instead of telling clergy, "You're insecure; that's why you became pastors," we should tell them, "Your insecurity is a vocation; it's an invitation to really live the spiritual life."

How can ministers accept their insecurity that way?

Nouwen: Here the spiritual director is important. You need a person with whom you feel free to be insecure. Let me paint a picture. You're in a big room with a six-inch balance beam in the center. The balance beam is only twelve inches off the fully carpeted floor. Most of us act as if we were blindfolded and trying to walk on that balance beam; we're afraid we'll fall off. But we don't realize we're only twelve inches off the floor. The spiritual director is someone who can push you off that balance beam and say, "See? It's okay. God still loves you. Take that nervousness about whether you're going to succeed and whether you have enough money — take the whole thing up on that narrow beam and just fall off."

Foster: That's one of the great values of reading the saints. They had this utter vulnerability to fail by human standards.

There seems to be a hunger among Christians for worship, both corporate and private. Why this thirst for spiritual things?

Foster: There's been a great disillusionment with the superficialities of modern culture, especially the religious culture, and a longing for something that can really help.

Nouwen: The churches in the United States, Catholic as well as Protestant, have never concentrated on the idea of spiritual formation. Pastoral care, yes, but a nurturing of the intimate life with God, no. The Catholic church was involved in getting herself established in the United States, building churches and schools. The Protestant church majored on bringing people together for fellowship — the place where you go with your pains and family struggles. There's a pastoral richness there that's good.

But the mystical (and that's a good word) has been short-changed in our culture by Catholic and Protestant alike. It's unfortunate, because in the Christian tradition there is an enormous treasury of this. If you study Luther, you find a spiritual life that most Lutherans are quite unfamiliar with. Wesley was deeply steeped in literature of the spritual life. Calvin quotes straight from the Desert Fathers.

Foster: Yes, many don't realize that the longest section in Calvin's *Institutes* is on prayer.

Nouwen: In the sixties we were concerned with social change; we learned change comes slowly at best, and it doesn't come at all without a spiritual grounding. The real protesters, the ones who are still protesting, receive their strength and inspiration not from social theorists but from the mystics. Jim Forrest, head of the International Fellowship of Reconciliation, came to see me last night. What did he talk about? He talked about Thomas Merton; he talked about prayer. We prayed more than we talked. Prayer gives him strength to continue to fight for a better world.

There is a Jewish story about a little boy who went to a prophet and said, "Prophet, don't you see? You have been prophesying now for fifteen years, and things are still the same. Why do you keep on?"

And the prophet said, "Don't you know, little boy, I'm not prophesying to change the world, but to prevent the world from changing me?"

We must say no to war, killing, and poverty, not because people are going to listen, but because it belongs to an authentic witness of the living God. And you can do that only when your heart is rooted in the love of God, not in the responses of the people. Maybe more people are seeing that and are saying to their ministers, "Tell me about the spiritual life. Tell me how to pray."

We've talked a lot about prayer. What is prayer?

Nouwen: Prayer is first of all listening to God. It's openness. God is always speaking; he's always doing something. Prayer is to enter into that activity. Take this room. Imagine you've never been out of it. Prayer is like going outside to see what's really there. Prayer in its most basic sense is just entering into an attitude of saying, "Lord, what are you saying to me?"

Foster: The problem with describing prayer as *speaking* to God is that it implies we are still in control. But in listening, we let go. Real intercession is what comes out of listening. People are tired of hearing about "ten steps that will change your life." That isn't where it's at, because then people tend to focus on the steps instead of hearing and obeying God.

The spiritual life is not something we add onto an already busy life. What we are talking about is to impregnate and infiltrate and control what we already do with an attitude of service to God. For pastors, this might mean silent prayer in their board meetings. One of the greatest revelations to me was to experiment with being in communion with God in board meetings. I learned I didn't always have to speak and control, and that I could pray for people in the room who had a heaviness with life. It's like living on two levels. On one you are doing the activities of the day, but on a deeper, more profound level, there is this inward prayer and worship.

What can we do to help us center our thoughts on God?

Foster: Many different things. My boys and I have built a basketball standard out by our driveway. I go out alone at ten at night and shoot baskets. It's a time to pray. And as I shoot baskets, I invite God to remind me of my day. Are there things that need to be confessed: Was I curt to my secretary? Do I need to set something straight? Am I disturbing my neighbors?

In the morning I've been having fun experimenting with prayer during that period of just starting to wake up. You aren't fully conscious, but you aren't fully asleep; during that in-between period I try to surrender my day to God.

Nouwen: People who live a spiritual life become sensitive to their surroundings. Notice their houses; they are uncluttered. Your physical place becomes more spacious when your life is lived spiritually. The idea of going on retreat for prayer is crucial, but we also need to pray daily. It's not only important to set aside time to pray, but also a place to pray. I have a special place to pray, and I spend a predetermined amount of time in this space. The only reason to be there is to pray. After the time is up I can say, "Lord, this was my prayer, even if my mind was full of confusion."

Foster: There are many practical ways to increase the spiritual atmosphere of the home. In our home we don't answer the telephone when we are eating or if I'm reading stories to the children, because I want my boys to know they are more important than the telephone.

Nouwen: The obvious assumption of always answering the phone is that the person on the phone has something more important to say than what you are saying, which is not true. The same applies to the television. My mother always said, "I don't understand why you tolerate this stranger talking in the middle of my room. We didn't invite him. Turn him off."

Foster: I have another suggestion for discipline that I have found very helpful. Tell people not only when a meeting starts, but when it ends. I don't mean only business meetings, but social meetings too. I always invite students from eight to ten in the evening. At ten I say, "Let's close with prayer."

Nouwen: A word here on the form of prayer. Prayer involves the body. It can be done in many different postures. You can stand, kneel, lie flat, hold hands, lie in bed, or sit in a chair.

Foster: You do what is appropriate for the type of prayer you are praying. A friend who is now a philosophy professor has prayed with me a great deal. I remember one time we met together to pray for some people in our congregation who had serious problems. As we began, my friend, who is over six feet tall, flattened himself straight out on the floor. I had planned to just kneel, but I realized his posture was appropriate for the kind of concern we had.

Nouwen: What is also important about different postures is that sometimes your mind is too tired to concentrate in the right way, and your body position can get you in the proper frame of mind.

What about the content of prayer?

Nouwen: Too many Christians think prayer means to have spiritual thoughts. That's not it. Prayer means to bring into the presence of God all that you are. You can say, "God, I hate this guy; I can't stand him." The prayer life of most people is too selective. They usually present only those things to God they want him to know or they think he can handle. But God can handle everything.

Foster: You've heard people say, "I don't know what to pray about." Or, they will get a prayer list and pray for missionaries because they don't know what else to do. A lady said to me not too long ago, "I can't pray for more than two minutes at a time. What can I do?" When people say that to me, I reply, "What have you been thinking or worrying about this last week? Pray about that."

Nouwen: Convert your thoughts into prayer. As we are involved in unceasing thinking, so we are called to unceasing prayer. The difference is not that prayer is thinking about other things, but that prayer is thinking in dialogue. It is a move from self-centered monologue to a conversation with God.

F O U R

MAINTAINING INTEGRITY UNDER PRESSURE

We should be asking ourselves constantly: Are power and leadership things I'm using to promote self, career, and prestige? Or are they being used only as a way of serving Christ?

MARK HATFIELD

Mark Hatfield

Referred to as "the conscience of the Senate," Mark O. Hatfield is serving his fourth term as Republican senator from Oregon. He is the second-ranking Republican in the Senate and is ranking minority member of the influential Senate Appropriations Committee. From 1980 to 1986 he served as chairman of that committee, the second-longest tenure in U.S. history.

As a lieutenant J.G. in the Navy, Hatfield commanded landing craft at Iwo Jima and Okinawa. He served in the Oregon State Legislature for six years, then became Oregon's secretary of state and later, governor for eight years.

Senator Hatfield holds the M.A. degree from Stanford University, as well as numerous honorary degrees, and is the author or coauthor of seven books, including Between a Rock and a Hard Place and Conflict and Conscience. As these titles reflect, Mark Hatfield has often felt the tension of being a committed Christian in the public arena. During his career he has cast a lone vote several times. In this conversation, the first in a section on the leader's personal challenges, he talks about how to maintain integrity under pressure.

You wrote *Between a Rock and a Hard Place*, so you've obviously done some thinking about this: What are the toughest pressures leaders face?

I would start with the pressures from our own egos. I think people of the pulpit and people of politics probably fight this problem to the same degree. Parishioners expect to see someone in the pulpit who has it all together. He or she's supposed to be the living example of Christlikeness. What a tremendous burden! What an impossible role we give our ministers when we expect them to be Christ.

In political life, you're not necessarily expected to be perfect, but you're expected to know all the answers. That's why you were elected.

How should we handle those expectations?

We have to accept that the expectations are there and do our best to live with them.

The real problem, though, is not the expectation but our ego, which sometimes makes us believe we are the ultimate model of spirituality. The original temptation, remember, was not to do evil but to do good: to eat the fruit and become like God. When our ego leads us up to that kind of pedestal, we're in trouble.

We need to pray we do not begin to believe what people think and say of us. I've found a good stabilizing measure is to form relationships of accountability. My wife and I belong to a group that includes the pastor of National Presbyterian Church and his wife, Louie and Coke Evans, and four other couples in Washington. We get together once a month and are accountable to each other. It's a ministry of support but also a ministry of accountability, which I think ministers need too.

I remember when I was governor for eight years, every few weeks I would have the name *George Smoka* on my calendar. He would come from the Union Gospel Mission and say with his commanding voice, "I've just come to pray for you, brother." With that he would raise his one hand toward the heavens and place the other on my shoulder, and he would simply pray. Then he'd say "Good-by; have a good day, brother." He'd walk out, and that was the extent of his call.

I always felt absolutely renewed and blessed by those calls. I think 90 percent of the people who called at my office were there for some request. But George Smoka never asked for a thing. That kind of support is invaluable for leaders.

You belong to probably the most exclusive club in the world, the United States Senate. In such a position, is humility more difficult to maintain?

Humility is unconscious. If you're conscious of your humility, then it isn't true humility. Humility is a manner, a viewpoint, an all-encompassing thing.

But humility is expressed through actions, say, a nod of the head in acknowledgment of a verbal hello. It can be demonstrated simply by stopping and listening to someone. Its essence is putting others ahead of yourself. By God's grace it can be demonstrated by anyone in any position. A pastor may show humility through offering a healing word to a hurting person.

A real test of humility is how you handle criticism. The natural reaction is to throw up an immediate defense, a quick excuse, a spontaneous rebuttal. The humble way to handle criticism is to try to understand the reasons for the criticism, to look for what truth there may be in it.

What other hazards must leaders watch for?

Power. Power is one of the most corruptive of all influences, so one should always look at power with a very jaundiced eye. We've seen in the history of the church the corruptive influences of power. And in individual churches there is a corruptive influence whenever a minister feels he has to be the controlling force of his congregation.

We all remember Jim Jones, who had utter control over congregations in California and Guyana. As I understand his background, he started out with the simple proclamation of the gospel. Then he began to sense a personal charismatic hold he had on people. It was a gift that was perverted and used for self-glory and promotion rather than for the Lord.

I admire Billy Graham's perspective. He is conscious of the fact he has achieved worldwide recognition, having proclaimed the gospel to more people than any other human being ever. He doesn't have the power of an ecclesiastical organization, but he has the power of influence and he recognizes its danger.

There's a fine line between motivation and manipulation, between the good and evil use of power. How do you discern the difference?

We should be asking ourselves constantly: Are power and leadership things I'm using to promote self, career, and prestige? Or are they being used only as a way of serving Christ and bringing people into a relationship with Christ? In other words, are we the masters or are we the servants?

We are not masters of the congregations or constituencies we lead; we are servants of such people. As we see our lives in that perspective, God can use us. But that's a constant battle, because the desire is always there to put self ahead, to take personal offense and let some issue rupture a relationship. I've often said my wife disagrees with me on many political issues. She cancels my vote in many elections, but that has not ruptured our relationship. It's not that a good relationship comes easily; we work at our relationship. We've learned, though, that when we personalize issues and consider challenges to issues as personal affronts, it is because our ego is emerging.

How do the pressures of leadership affect your relationship with your family?

The home is the toughest environment of all for leaders. Why is it the ones we love most are the ones we are the most impatient with? My wife has often said to me, "I wish you were as patient with your children as you are with your constituents." She's right. She reminds me that I'm accountable to God and to my family, and I'm grateful for that.

I think the greatest problem we have is our allocation of time, whether or not we let our professions work to the exclusion of our families. If our lives are going to be given only to our professions, then better we had remained as Paul said, unencumbered by marriage and family. But if we do decide to marry and have a family, I am thoroughly convinced one has to set priorities as follows:

Our first priority is to God. The Bible teaches us to "love the Lord thy God with all thy strength, mind, and heart."

Our second priority is to our family, because they are the gift of God to us; they are the joint effort of God's creating authority working through us.

Our third priority is our profession, and if we put our job any place higher than third place, we have our priorities askew.

So it takes a lot of understanding on the part of the leader's family, and a lot of understanding on the part of the leader. I've tried to communicate to my family that no matter how busy I am, I am always accessible to them. That has to be communicated verbally, but also in action.

In the midst of these pressures, what is your task as a leader? What must a leader actually do?

Three things. First, the leader must demonstrate commitment to the goals, objectives, and spirit of the program or organization he is leading. That commitment cannot be half-hearted; it has to be a total commitment.

Second, the leader must translate the institution's objectives into the lives of followers. A leader must make the objectives relevant and helpful for people, and show he genuinely cares for them.

Third, a leader always has to be alert to change. The Bible teaches that Jesus Christ is the same yesterday, today, and forever, and the pastor's message contains a continuity of truth. But that does not mean conditions around that truth are not changing. Cultural changes, social changes, and political changes affect every person and institution, and a leader has to recognize change and adapt, so that he or she never loses relevancy.

Whom do you admire as a leader? Who does these things well?

I wouldn't have to think for a second to say Richard Halverson, chaplain of the Senate.

Dick came to the Senate at a time when the Republicans had just taken control. Because he was a Wheaton College graduate, Princeton Seminary graduate, and Presbyterian pastor, there was a little bit of political tension, as you can imagine. Yet into that situation came this man who met first with the pages, then the elevator operators, and then the capitol police. He visited each senator personally, and then he talked to their spouses to indicate his interest in serving them. It's amazing the way this man has developed a shepherding role for the so-called up-and-outers, and what a response he's received from the Senate.

Each session opens with prayer, and many senators used to absent themselves from the floor because it was one of those routine acts that people felt a little bored with. Now, most of us come to at least read his sermon or prayer because it's always so relevant to who we are and what we are doing.

For example, one Christmas Dick prayed, "Father, help us to be mindful that you did not announce the Incarnation of your Son to the Roman Senate, but to a few lowly shepherds out on the hillside." Another time, we were in a late session and tensions were high. He prayed at the midnight hour (which was the beginning of a new day and a new session), "Humpty Dumpty sat on a wall; Humpty Dumpty had a great fall. All the king's horses and all the king's men couldn't put Humpty Dumpty together again. Father, help the Senate to stick together." Still another time he prayed that God would help the senators understand that when they are home they are not senators but spouses and parents: "Help them not to treat their families they way they've treated their staffs."

The *New York Times* and *Washington Post* have commented editorially on Dick's prayers, and out of those helpful, pertinent prayers has developed the kind of pastoral role the senators have learned to rely on in times of family crisis. One lost his grandson in a terrible tragedy. He made funeral arrangements and asked Dick to travel to his home state to preach the eulogy for his grandson, whom Dick had never met.

So your model of a Christian leader is someone who can speak authoritatively but simply and lovingly, too.

Yes, a person who is so vulnerable he makes you vulnerable. Unwittingly, and perhaps unconsciously, we sometimes feel our title, our position, and our responsibilities mean we *have* to perform in the exact manner expected of us. In so doing we dehumanize ourselves.

Being vulnerable means we are standing totally open as a human being — not as a pastor, not as a senator, not as a leader, not as a follower — just a human being. And there is nothing that elicits response from people more than to feel they are dealing with someone who is on their level — who feels what they feel.

Can someone who isn't especially people oriented become an effective leader?

I know of days when even Dick Halverson has found it difficult to be in one-to-one relationships with people. He has shared that when he was a pastor, he spent much of his time in the pulpit or preparing to exposit the Scriptures, and he found casual conversation was not his cup of tea. Realizing this, he said, "I am more and more aware that Christ living in you is what really creates the ability to be sensitive and responsive to people."

Overall, what's your goal as a leader?

To apply in practical ways the servant leadership that Christ represented. That's not always easy, but I don't think the Lord taught anything to his followers that is not achievable.

Christ did not say, "Come and follow me, but you'll never really make it because I'm God and you aren't."

I sometimes feel great pressures as a leader. Those pressures tempt us to shortchange areas in our lives. But if we have integrity, we can live whole, integrated lives. We can't say, "This is my public life, and this is my private life; these are my public morals, these my private morals." What we are, we are. If that is a person of integrity, then it will show through in every setting.

F I V E

UNDERSTANDING YOUR ROLE IN THE SYSTEM

My responsibility is to be a supervisor, not a superworker.

FRED SMITH

Fred Smith

H

ave you noticed that the simplest, most fundamental questions can be the most difficult to answer? Anyone who's raised small children knows the challenge of defining the basics. Try answering "What's gravity, Daddy?"

Leaders, too, may be tripped up by the fundamentals: What am I to do? Of the many things that need to be done in this church or organization, what few belong to me? In short, what is my role?

One person who communicates these fundamentals of leadership clearly is Fred Smith.

Fred cannot be easily described. He is a businessman, consultant, public speaker, active Christian. Even meetings become interesting when Fred is in them. He has an unusual ability to pinpoint the real issue, to cut through the undergrowth.

When Fred was forty, he turned down the presidency of a national corporation so he could divide his attention among business, education, religion, and lecturing. He has served on more than twenty boards and trusteeships, holds an honorary doctor of laws degree, and was awarded the Lawrence Appley award of the American Management Association.

While he truly enjoys business, he keeps reaching out for the broader life. For many years he was active in the leadership of Laymen's Leadership Institute. Fred has served as chairman of the national board of Youth for Christ, and as a member of the executive committee of Christianity Today, Inc. He was chairman for Billy Graham's earliest Cincinnati crusade. He has been consultant to such corporations as GENESCO, Mobil, and Caterpillar, and has lectured in over twenty universities and forty-six states and foreign countries.

Fred is also a contributing editor of LEADERSHIP *Journal and the author of* You and Your Network *(Word) and* Learning to Lead *(Leadership/Word).*

You have achieved a great deal in your life. How did you find the time?

Those of us who divide our efforts, particularly in the more visible activities, may appear to do more, but I doubt we really do. Frankly, I thought you might ask me why I have done so little, considering what Wesley, Napoleon, Churchill, et al., have done with the same twenty-four hours. I keep thinking how much Wesley did and how he was dead for several years before he was my age.

Fred, you always appear relaxed, even casual, yet there is below the surface a lurking intensity.

Intensity is the boiling point of effort, the concentration of energy, the tip of the welding flame. Most men of accomplishment have a special ability to develop intensity at the right time over the right issue.

Jackie Robinson could come out of his relaxed pose at second base and snap into action as the play came to him, then go back into a poised relaxation, saving himself for the next time. Most pros have this; only the amateur keeps jumping up and down like a college cheerleader. Many hardworking people fail to accomplish much because they lack intensity at the meaningful time.

Good leadership picks out the crucial elements and places something extra at these points.

Can you describe your approach to leadership?

Yes. It involves a few concepts plus techniques, most of which I've borrowed from those I admire. Of course, I've adapted these to my personal style.

I like to find the essence of each situation, like a logger clearing a log jam. The pro climbs a tall tree and locates the key log, blows it, and lets the stream do the rest. An amateur would start at the edge of the jam and move all the logs, eventually moving the key log. Both approaches work, but the "essence" concept saves time and effort. Almost all problems have a "key log" if we learn to find it.

I try to decide what I'm trying to do, what it takes to do it, and whom I can get to do it better than I can. I find summary thoughts helpful in keeping me conscious of my concepts, such as, "Results are the only reason for activity."

What is your role in this leadership system?

I use this definition: "An executive is not a person who can do the work better than his people; he is a person who can get his people to do the work better than he can." My responsibility is to be a super*visor*, not a super*worker*. A little selective laziness is not all bad. It increases the thinking time.

It is very important that the people who work for me understand *my* job. If they don't know what my job is, they often try to do it. That's why it's so important for them to know what I want to retain control of. I decide this very simply. I make a list of all the things that only I can do. It's an embarrassingly short list. I have to add a few things that I prefer doing to make the list long enough to justify my salary. It's amazing how few things there are that only the boss can do.

Most bosses don't think this way. They say, "How much can I do? Whatever I can't do I'll hire someone else to do." Well, that's the way you work yourself to death.

I was talking to an Oklahoma bank president who said he was working himself to death. I said, "Whose work are you doing?"

He stopped, reflected for a moment, and answered, "Well, to be honest, the cashier's."

I asked, "Why are you doing it?"

He said, "I hadn't really thought it through. I'm going to go back and straighten out that situation."

Your system requires competent people who will get the job done.

Yes. If you don't understand selection, development, and motivation, you will suffer by this system.

For example, recently I looked at an organization with problems. I asked the board, "Is our lead horse strong enough to pull the wagon?"

They said no.

"Okay," I said, "where is the one we need?" So we went out and found a strong man and turned the organization around. I could have approached it differently. I could have said, "This man we have here is a sincere, fine Christian person, and with enough help he just might do it." But that would have meant pulling with him for five years before we found out he couldn't do the job. We would have used up a tremendous amount of time and effort and paralyzed the organization just to avoid a tough decision.

The earlier you make a decision about a failure and "cut your loss," the less actual waste. People who wait around trying to find the pleasant, comfortable moment to make difficult decisions and difficult changes are simply kidding themselves. You can hide behind "We're going to wait and pray about it," but when you *know* the situation is going wrong, then do something to alleviate it. The answer to most problems is the right people in the right places.

How would you respond to a pastor who says, "That's all right for bosses and presidents, but all I have is a secretary and some volunteers. Delegation is out of the question."

As long as you have one other person in your organization, you can be learning delegation. Delegation is a philosophy before it is a practice. Some parents do everything for the children, while others teach the children to do for themselves. I don't know many churches as small as a family.

Most leaders who don't delegate want others to be dependent on them; they want to be needed more than they want to develop their associates. Be sure you don't try to delegate the "dirty" part of the job and keep the good part. "Folks ain't dumb."

The pastor who is doing everything himself might ask, "Aren't there pastors who lead small churches who don't work themselves to death, who don't handle all of the details?" Then the next question would be, "Are their members different from mine?" Well, most members are about the same wherever you go. This begins to make him believe there's something about management that he doesn't understand.

For the pastor who feels swamped with committee meetings and administrative work, what do we say to help him or her break out of this trap?

I would say, "Be honest about why you're swamped." If you're protecting your job by being sure you're in the center of everything, it's your own fault. If you just have a natural curiosity about what's going on, and you like to be with people, and you're spending your time with people and details instead of studying and praying, it's your fault. If you're insecure and cannot let other people take responsibility, it's your fault. I can't accept the premise that there is a job big enough to keep me away from my primary responsibilities.

Andrew Carnegie once asked a consultant, "What can you do for me about time control?"

The consultant said, "I'll make one suggestion, and you send me a check for what you think it's worth. Write down what you have to do on a piece of paper in order of priority, and complete the first item before you go to the second." It's reported that Carnegie tried it for a few weeks and sent him a check for ten thousand dollars.

I constantly find people trying to accomplish their work as if they were eating dinner at a smorgasbord. They don't prioritize anything and they don't complete anything. They don't practice good time discipline. I had an executive say to me, "How in the world do you turn down people who want to play golf with you?" That question has never entered my mind. My time is as much mine as my money. If I don't let everybody else spend my money, I'm not going to let them spend my time. I have a right and a responsibility to say to people, "I have to have this much time for my priorities."

For example, I was traveling with the president of a subsidiary company, and every time we'd sit down anywhere he'd grab a big stack of magazines and start reading them. I asked, "Do you like to read?"

He said, "I hate to."

"But every time I'm with you, you spend your time reading. Why do you do that?"

He said, "The president of the parent company sends me these magazines."

I said, "What would happen if you'd walk into the president's office and say, 'Hey, Boss, you want me to make money or read magazines? I'm willing to do either one, but I can't read all these magazines you're sending me and do my job too'? I will guarantee the boss would laugh and say, 'Throw those magazines in the basket. I sent them to you because I thought they were too current to throw away.' " A lot of people will generate work for you on this same basis.

A man came in to see me who had written a book and brought a copy for me to read — a big, thick book. He said, "I'll call you in a week and see what you think about my book."

I said, "Make it six months. This book costs $10.90. Since I'm a slow reader, it would take me two days to read it. That means I'd be making about $5.45 a day reading your book, and I think I'm worth more than that." Unless a book has something to do with what I'm trying to learn, and I consider it a priority, I'm not going to read it just so someone can call me and say, "What did you think about the book?" I'm going to be frank and say I don't read books just because people give them to me.

But a pastor might say, "I'm a public person. My congregation expects to be able to telephone me day or night. They shove books under my nose and next Sunday ask me about them. My job is to minister to these people, to get to know them and build rapport with them. As irritating as these requests for 'personal favors' are, a response is necessary."

This sounds like the politician who spends all his time running for office and never performs when he gets in. Building rapport can be a smoke screen. The pastor must set some time aside for it, but he must constantly remind people of his commitment to the most important things. I don't think they would be offended the least bit if he said, "Folks, Tuesday is my day with God. I have to spend some time with my boss to keep this job, and he has called me into conference on Tuesday. He takes a dim view of me answering phones and appearing at social occasions on conference day. Your boss wouldn't like it if you ran out of the room when he was trying to talk to you. Mine doesn't either."

I know a pastor who does this. He simply shuts himself off from his people on Tuesday so he can study. But they all know he's studying. I know a life insurance man who refuses all social engagements on a certain evening because he wants to be a well-versed insurance man. No one invites him anywhere on that night because they know he's studying life insurance. He has become a veritable authority, and being known for studying one night a week has helped his reputation.

A minister must explain what he is supposed to be doing for his people. He is supposed to be expounding the Word to them. He can't expound without studying. If he's going to let secondary matters take over, no matter how important they might be, he would be like the merchant who was so bent on trying to keep the store clean he would never unlock the front door. The real reason for running the store is to have customers come in, not to clean it up.

We find this in Parkinson's Law — if you have only one letter to write, it will take all day to do it. If you have twenty letters to do, you'll get them done in one day. The most efficient time of life is the week before vacation. Why can't we run our lives as we do the week before vacation — make decisions, clean off the desk, return the calls? Take the use of a secretary. If I want people to deal with my secretary on important matters, I must build her up to where they feel she's capable. Therefore, every once in a while, I'll say, "You'll find she is great on that; in fact, she's better at that than I am." And they will feel it is an honor to deal with her. But she has to be good. You can't kid about it.

The pastor who wants somebody else to do visitation had better use sermon illustrations about the great things that have happened because someone else does the visiting. If illustrations are only about when the pastor visited, the congregation will expect that presence.

But doesn't the average congregation expect the pastor to carry the ball on visitation as well as preaching?

One time I became interested in trying to find a job in the Bible like our preacher has. You can't find one like the modern preacher to save your life. We don't have a scriptural setup. We have one that's grown up out of tradition. And I'm not too sure that ministers haven't developed it themselves. Like everyone else, they reached for more and more authority, more and more prestige, more and more power, and created for themselves a job nobody can do. It takes an absolute genius to adequately do the pastor's job.

One morning I thought, *What if today I were a pastor instead of a corporation president?* That idea scared me to death. I am totally inadequate to fulfill the job most pastors have.

In other conversations you've alluded to three different organizational systems. Could you talk about them?

I call them the *poor human system,* the *good human system,* and the *spiritual system.* I've had a great deal of experience with the poor human system and some with the good human system; not until rather recently did I see a different type of church management that intrigued me. I've been studying it — not fully understanding it — but seeing there is a difference, not in degree but in kind.

Describe these three systems.

I can give you some identifying marks. This is personal opinion that comes from observing and participating in many churches for over fifty years.

Most churches are run on the poor human system, a kind of system you'd run a marginal business with. In a marginal church you have a "Mom and Pop" operation that the pastor and his wife are running. The church will not pay Mom, although they expect her to work. She runs the missionary society, helps with the catering, makes calls with Pop, and usually plays the organ. If she's really strong, she may teach a class and even quietly help him prepare the sermon. Though she is not paid, she comes under the same review as Pop. These Mom-and-Pop operations never grow very big because Mom and Pop have to see and do everything.

Some insidious things usually start to happen. Mom and Pop often learn to like this management style and they become attached to the location, or at least they don't know another place to go. And, being human, security becomes important to them.

Now, what happens? Mom and Pop inadvertently form a small clique. They want a hand in who is on the board of deacons, who is doing everything — even the janitoring, so the janitor will tell them what he heard from the members who didn't know he was listening. This control system is initiated out of desire for security. It is one of the most limiting factors that can exist in an organization. Directly or indirectly, many smaller churches are controlled by Mom and Pop, and you'll find they come in varying degrees of attractiveness. Sometimes Mom and Pop are great. Sometimes they fight with each other. Sometimes they are a wonderful team.

The poor human system is a management style, a style that can be spotted the moment you walk in the front door. Pop leads the singing, makes the announcements, prays the prayer, preaches the sermon, pronounces the benediction, and runs down the aisle to shake hands with the people at the door. He does everything — just like a small businessman — because it is *his* little operation. It's the only system he knows. And God bless Mom and Pop! A vast number of Christians would not be blessed if they didn't exist.

I've often wanted to sit down and say to them, "Do you know there's another system? Do you know there's a way to do all this and not work yourself to death?"

Lay people help perpetrate this human system. They enjoy the familiarity with Mom and Pop. It helps them know where their place is in the congregational mix. They like the paternalistic, benevolent feel that comes from Mom and Pop, and they develop their own form of "clout" by being part of Mom and Pop's family.

We have to be careful when we talk about the poor human system in a church. Poor human system doesn't mean poor Christian experience. Some of the finest, most meaningful Christian experiences one can possibly have will be found in a church run by poor human administration.

But if the poor human system is so inefficient and security oriented, how can you say the most meaningful Christian experiences possible can come out of this kind of environment?

Remember, when I say system, I'm talking about the administrative system; I'm not talking about theology or Spirit. We must make the distinction. There is no system by which humans can accomplish what only God can do. One of the great failures of the church is that we often try to accomplish with a human system (good or bad) what only God can do.

For example, we cannot accomplish with a revival activity or renewal program the salvation of souls. Whenever we substitute people walking down an aisle or numerical growth for spiritual transformation, we're trying to do through a human system what cannot be done.

Regardless of the system, one of the most important things to learn is to delegate to God. If I were a minister, one of the first things I would declare is that God is my boss. My boss could not be the chairman of the board. The day I genuinely quit believing God was my boss, I'd get out of the ministry.

Of course, this too has problems. God is often viewed as an absentee boss. Branch offices get into trouble when there's an absentee manager. Some corporate officers get carried away and do very self-serving things that get the company into trouble because the stockholders are absentee owners. The closer the relationship between the owner and the manager, the better the place will be run. In the same way, the more God's presence is felt in any church, the better it will be run. The quality of spiritual blessing comes not from the system, but from God.

Describe the good human system.
The key to a good human system is a dynamic leader. This is a person who could make it in business, ministry, or almost anything. He has that rare combination of abilities to preach, teach, and administer. When I say good human system, I'm talking about good human management, the kind that can be taught through an MBA program.

What are the characteristics of this system?
Good human managers understand organization. They understand human nature. For example, Napoleon's strength was that he understood what men would do in war. A good human system preacher understands what people will do in a religious context. Thus he knows how to motivate them. A good human leader understands that any successful operation is run by a small oligarchy, and that the oligarchy is controlled by one man. Egotism plays a big part in the human system.

You're saying he understands power?
He understands how things get done! He doesn't argue with it or philosophize about it; he accepts it. He isn't always apologizing, "Well, I hate to get things done this way, but . . . " He knows how to utilize people's strengths and buttress their weaknesses. He knows that people don't basically change: People enthusiastically do what they can do well, and drag their feet on what they can't do well.

The good human system requires that you divide work into its logical parts. Then, you put somebody in charge who has the capability of doing it. When a good human leader starts using a new person, he always *assigns* rather than *delegates* to him. Assigning means telling him what you want, what time you want it, and how you want it done. And you expect him to do it himself while you watch the task get done. As you develop experience with this person, you find there are certain things you can delegate to him. Delegating is the second step; you simply tell him what problem you'd like to have solved and he develops and implements the solution. *But you must have working experience with somebody in order to move from assignment to delegation.* I've seen people who bypassed the assignment process, delegated prematurely, and then damned the delegation system. We have all seen new Christians, particularly wealthy or famous ones, hurt by overuse before they mature. God can wait for them to mature; it's the rest of us who get overanxious to use them in our programs.

How do power and authority work in the good human system?

In the good human system your capacity to organize is often based upon the recognized authority you possess.

On one level you have people who feel God has endowed them in such a special way they can tell people what to do. People are to be subordinate to them whether they will admit it or not.

Another kind of authority is given authority. You give a man a title or an office. The title carries a certain authority. It's probably the most vulnerable kind of authority because people will often subtly test it. If all he has is the title of authority, pretty soon the testing will produce a breakdown, and that person will be forced to compromise.

Then you have authority by means of dedication. In any organization those who are the most dedicated have a tendency to rise to levels of authority, even though it may be behind-the-scenes authority. They work harder and stay longer.

Superior knowledge is a form of authority. If you know more than anybody in the group, they will turn to you. But the moment somebody with superior knowledge enters the scene, you lose all of your authority to that person. That's why the pastor has to be careful about building authority on a superior knowledge of a theme in the Bible; it can be lost if a better teacher or a more dramatic theme comes along.

Franklin D. Roosevelt had the image of providing benefits for people. This gave him unparalleled political power. The people wanted him to be their four-term boss because they could expect good things from him. Few preachers can give things, but they can overdo "good feelings" and develop authority over many.

I like to write on paper the basis of my authority. If I own a business, people recognize my ownership rights. But if I don't watch it, if I'm not exercising my ownership function, somebody will try to take it over. Squatters are not all poor. There are squatters on unoccupied authority. I have seen choirs form a "squatters' rights" clique.

The way Henry Ford lost control of the Ford Foundation.

Owning something doesn't mean you're going to remain in authority. In fact, one of the perils of the good human system is related to ownership. Ownership may mean you can throw others out, but then you're faced with the terrible problem of how you're going to run the system once they are gone.

One of the German philosophers told me that Hitler came to power in a power vacuum. There came that pause when nobody wanted to run the place. He was the only one who did, and everyone else said, "Let him." As soon as he was in power, he set up the means to keep others from challenging him.

I don't believe a Christian can have a conscience for that kind of power. But in the church I've seen key people get tired of serving in major capacities (and they all seem to get tired at the same time), and suddenly mediocre people are in power simply because the others defaulted. Power is not an inert thing. It's like mercury; it flows. A capable leader, like a good coach, looks to the bench for continuity in winning.

How would you summarize the good human system?

Motivation in the good human system is identical to the motivation used in any other successful human process. Participation, recognition, rotation, the feeling of belonging, moving up through the ranks — all of these principles are the same anywhere.

Rotation?

Right. A person gets tired of teaching one grade level so you move him to another grade level so he won't lose interest in teaching. If a person's tired of being on one committee, you put him on another committee to keep him excited. Also, you protect the organization by rotation. You keep someone from sitting in a job until he thinks he owns it.

Privately, the men I know in the good human system are very candid with their close associates. However, they take a long time to move a person into the inside group. Former governor of Texas John Connally once said, "I have very few close friends and I take a long time to make one." What he may be saying is, "There are parts to my life or organization I don't want anyone to see until I trust them."

Good human leaders are lonely, but they don't necessarily try to avoid loneliness; they accept it as part of the price. I mentioned this one time to the president of an architectural firm, and he said, "You've just identified all my problems. Because I hate to be lonely and I'm always telling my associates about my half-baked plans, bad things begin to happen to me." He didn't realize that everyone who would be helped by his half-baked plan began to support it, and everyone who would be hurt by it started to work against it — before it was even formulated! Confusion and polarization were born out of his desire to talk.

In the good human system, people who share everything with everybody tend to be less than great leaders. Most great leaders appear open, but are often closed. In fact, in the good human system, hypocrisy is often a requirement. This is one of the reasons I do not feel it is a system that God would prefer to use. For example, if the leader wanted Deacon Smith removed, he would publicly shed great tears about the "trouble" in the body, and how the Lord had helped him to identify this problem, and how the Lord needed to help him help these "people." Invoking the Lord is a smoke screen. It is the good human system working in its best and worst fashion. And this is the hypocrisy that bothers me. But keep in mind that I'm convinced that God is going to use whatever system is around. I think this is part of his sovereignty. I also think it is part of his humor. Remember the old saw, "God can use any kind of vessel except a dirty one"? Well, from my experience, that is the only kind he can use. We are all sinners.

The motivations in the good human system are absolutely human. The politics are human. You bring in the people that you can count on. You never let a person into the inner circle until you have his vote in your pocket. You never take a chance on a person who might vote on an issue as he sees it. The system admits a person who will question the issue but is sure to vote with the group. Questioning the issue is a safeguard, but you don't take a chance of him voting against you. After he does that once or twice, he's out.

Wait a minute! This is a description of how good and great leaders lead?

I'm not saying "great" leaders. There are those with solidness of character, strength of spirit, and dedication to a cause. They are the great exceptions we all long to follow but see so seldom. I know the danger of naming anyone, but it helps to personify types. Whenever I have been around Hudson Armerding, the former president of Wheaton College, he has impressed me as a man who truly wants to be a good man. Most of us want to be recognized as good, but few truly want to pay the price. In corporate life Howard Pew approached this type, as did Maxey Jarman. I feel safe in naming these men because each would have castigated me for putting him up as an example. Those who would enjoy being named are like the man who won an award for humility, and then when he wore it had it taken away from him.

I believe God wants to get us as close to maturity as he possibly can. Here in America we are basing a great deal of our

Christian success on the good human system — a system taken right out of industry and entertainment. In many cases ministers could be replaced with non-Christian executives. This scares me.

What are your views on the spiritual system?
While the good human system is based upon a dynamic, highly motivated, competent leader, the spiritual system is built *around* — not *upon* — a shepherd, whose purpose is to develop mature Christians, not a facility, a memorial, or a human organization. He looks at a facility as helpful but not vital. Organization is a part of the process for himself as well as for the flock.

In human systems the individual leader doesn't tend to mature spiritually because his purpose mitigates against spiritual maturity. In the maneuvering and the manipulations and the passing out of the accolades, the human system leader is forced to claim more spiritual maturity than he has.

That's sobering. It could be a trap for any of us.
Spiritual system leaders push the dynamics of growth and leadership toward their people for the people's benefit, rather than pull from the people the dynamics of "growth and leadership" that will ultimately benefit themselves.

You watch a human system leader, and he will often slowly start to satisfy his ego off the organization instead of sacrificing his ego to the organization. He eventually comes to that dangerous turning point where he goes from cause orientation to self orientation. When he begins his leadership he may be very cause oriented, but as he sees the cause prosper he starts to embezzle from the cause — either praise, credit, position, or money. The things that should have gone to God, he starts to take. Once he starts this process his commission begins to climb and soon he has gone from 1 percent to 15 percent to 50 percent. In extreme cases he finally says, "Well, God doesn't really need it, and since I'm God's man, I'll just take it all." Thank God these people are few in number.

Fred, you've been coming down hard on the leader. Isn't it possible he gets caught in the momentum of the system?

Of course this is possible. However, he can't effectively lead any system unless he has a natural tendency, understanding, and love for that system.

The human system is built on ego. For example, it almost always removes time for meditation and time for God. When you talk to many of these human system leaders, they sincerely decry their need for more time to pray and study the Bible. These leaders have a great tendency to never find this kind of time because of "the system." They have committees to attend and meetings to run.

But the leader of the spiritual system is different. By definition, he is not an administrator. He's a shepherd. The shepherd is involved in administration, but it's one of the functions of the church, not his personal function. He knows how many sheep there are, and he is prepared to take drastic action if one is missing. But his function does not revolve around personal power. A function that is saturated with responsibility is very different from a function that is saturated with power.

A pastor told me he was going to Africa with his staff, and I asked him how many he was going to take. He said, "All of them. All the personnel — eleven ministers."

I said, "Who's going to run the church?"

He said, "The same lay people who are running it when we're here."

His job wasn't to run the church. His job was to minister to people. I don't know of many human systems that could stand the strain of every paid worker being gone for six weeks. The place would fold.

When I speak to American Management Association meetings, I can always tell the insecure corporate presidents whose offices have not called as often as they would like. They are scared to death the business is running without them. You find parents like this — scared to death the kids are going to get along without them.

The spiritual system utilizes people by their gifts. Its function is ministry and its object is maturation. The church's vitality cannot be measured in the number of meetings, the number of people, or the things that can be accomplished by human means. The church cannot be evaluated by any human scale.

So the spiritual system is built upon the gifts of the people *around* a pastor rather than *upon* the pastor. What would that look like?

Do you mean a church that isn't a pyramid with the senior pastor on top? I think some of the things Ray Stedman is doing, maybe unconsciously, have a tendency to accomplish this. For example, he leans away from building a sanctuary large enough to accommodate the entire membership, because he wants them to meet all over town. A church large enough to accommodate everyone at 11 A.M. would help to create a pyramid with a visible peak.

Another way to help prevent the development of a pyramid structure would be to develop ministers who do not have specialized functions. If four men share the preaching, you break some of the "pecking order."

When I read Ray's book, *Body Life*, I didn't think it was a complete statement of what went on. While riding with Ray to an airport I said, "You left the heart out of *Body Life*. What you have written won't work."

Naturally Ray was surprised, and he said, "I tried to be honest."

You can't make Ray defensive, which to me is one of the saintly qualities. "What you have left out is what most of us can't do," I told him. "You have gained control of your ego. And without control of your ego, the Body Life system won't work."

I have a suspicion that at some time in Ray's life he dedicated his ego to God. This is not saying Ray isn't human. It's simply saying I believe he has come to the place of saying, "This ministry is God's."

For a moment assume the perspective of a pastor. What kind of relationship would you try to establish with the lay leadership of the church?

It's very difficult for me to project myself into the ministerial role. One of the things I've been grateful for is that I have never really felt called. I'm sure there are churches that are grateful for the same thing!

If I were pastor of a church, I would have to take as my first concern the spiritual vitality of the leadership, not the political vitality. I would try to see that the lay leadership took seriously what we together claim to profess.

As a pastor I would also ask the lay leaders to be monitors of my spiritual vitality. I would appreciate it if one of my leaders came to me and said, "Pastor, I sense that you're a little low. I came to pray with you. May I read the Scripture with you?"

When you are close enough to your lay leadership for them to talk to you about your spiritual vitality, and you to talk to them about theirs — that would be the heart of a successful church operated on a spiritual basis.

S I X

EVALUATING PERSONAL PERFORMANCE

The greatest resource for self-evaluation is openness, the quality of being open with elders, staff, and spouse.

GENE GETZ

Gene Getz

Self-evaluation in ministry has a built-in dilemma: Effective ministry demands a certain absence of self-consciousness, yet evaluating ministry demands self-awareness.

It takes an unusual person to do this. Gene Getz is just such an unusual person; he's both an activist and an analyst. After teaching Christian education and directing the evening school at Moody Bible Institute in Chicago, he moved to Dallas Theological Seminary in Texas.

"This was during the anti-institutional era of the late sixties, and I had students asking tough questions like 'Who needs the church?' " says Getz. His defense of the church and what it should be eventually became a book — Sharpening the Focus of the Church. But then he was challenged to put his theories into practice.

In 1972, with approximately eight couples, he started Fellowship Bible Church. Within a year, the church was holding double services, and Getz had to choose between being full-time professor or full-time pastor. He opted for the pastorate.

Branch churches began to sprout, and four years later, in 1977, Getz himself left the home base to pastor the Park Cities branch.

Currently fourteen Fellowship Bible Churches are ministering in the Dallas area. Getz is pastor of Fellowship Bible Church North in Plano as well as director of the Center for Church Renewal.

How can a Christian leader tell if he or she is doing a good job? What are the signs that things are going well?

The first sign is spiritual growth. Are people responding spiritually? Are lives being changed?

Second, if there is potential, there should be numerical growth. There are areas with little potential for growth, but in most cases, no growth means something is wrong.

Third, is there unity around biblical principles? If you're all going the same direction and the leadership team is committed to the same goals — not just because the pastor is, but because their hearts are committed — that unity offers tremendous spiritual power.

I believe good leadership means communicating values, helping people internalize them, and allowing the body to respond.

What about the pastor's personal life? Is personal discontent, for example, an indication that something is wrong?

That can work two ways. The pastor's attitude can be *affected by* the congregation's health, or the attitude can *affect* the life of the church. Pastoral discontent, for example, can be contagious, injecting a negative mentality.

In one church where I was a member (not pastor), I remember thinking if I heard the word *commitment* one more time, I'd regurgitate. During each sermon, the congregation was "beaten," made to feel horribly guilty. The pastor was creating a neurotic, angry church.

One Sunday afternoon, I told my wife, "I predict that someday we'll hear that man confess from the pulpit that lack of commitment is a problem in his own life." I suspected the theme was a projection of his own needs.

Sure enough, two years later he admitted he was preaching out of weakness in the area of commitment. He left the church because of statements about his relationship with another woman.

What resources for self-evaluation does the leader have?

The greatest resource is openness, the quality of being open with elders, staff, and spouse. They can tell you if you're doing a good job — as long as you've created a climate where they can also say, "We've got a problem here" or "You've offended someone, and you need to be aware of it" or "You're preaching too long, and the services are cramped."

A second resource is the ability to keep your ear to the ground. How are people responding? Watch body language as you speak, and you can tell if people trust you, if they feel you're exhorting them because you love them or if they feel you're angry, being unfair, or manipulating them.

An absence of criticism should not be your goal in ministry, though I admit criticism is always painful for me. Lack of criticism means one of two things: You're doing such a good job no one can complain, or you've got people intimidated, afraid to speak up. The latter leads to criticism behind your back — a far more dangerous situation than being criticized directly.

How do you sort out fair criticisms from unfair?

One couple left our church, and when I visited them, they claimed they left because we promoted the building program too much in the major services. I didn't think it was true, but I try not to be the kind of leader who assumes critics are wrong. I needed some perspective.

First, I talked it over with our staff, attempting to weigh the issue objectively.

Second, I tried to quantify the issue and discovered we had made three public presentations in the last year — all in a context of worship and praise.

Third, I discussed my findings with the couple as non-defensively as I could. After listening carefully and trying to understand them, I was surprised and pleased when one of them confessed, "We may be the 'weaker brethren' in this situation because in this affluent society, we don't have the money to contribute that other people do."

So I learned to be aware that a hidden and possibly unrecognized agenda might be at work. In this case, the couple didn't feel comfortable because they couldn't do what other people were doing. I told them we wanted them back, but I would pray for God's blessing on them whatever decision they made.

The couple has not returned. But they did say, "This is the first time in our church experience that a pastor has come out to listen to us and tell us he loved us."

This situation was hard on me, because previously I had thought this couple was committed to the church 150 percent. It was a shock to see the intensity of their feelings over a seemingly minor issue.

So anyone can have a sore point, and if you inadvertently hit it, the person is going to react.

We need to remember that's true of us as well.

Recently a fellow handed me a letter with several points of criticism. Most of them I could handle, but the final point hit me at the wrong time, and the way it was phrased touched one of my own sore points, an area where I'd been painfully attacked before.

I reacted sharply — "I'm with you through point five, but when you hit point six, you don't know what you're talking about!" Later, after talking it over with an associate, I realized the critic somewhat innocently hit my emotional flash point.

So in weighing criticism, it's important to ask, *Is this touching an area that's emotional nitroglycerin for me?* If so, I need to be extra careful and rely on the judgments of trusted friends.

Tell us about a criticism you realized was valid. How did you change?

I'll give you three examples.

A few years ago, before church one Sunday, I was hurrying around and saw a young man and said, "Hi, how are you doing?" I kept walking.

An elder stopped me ten steps later and said, "Gene, you just did something I do — you didn't hear that kid. You asked how he was doing, and he said, 'Not so good.' You didn't stay around long enough to hear his reply."

I went back to the young man and apologized. He told me his brother had just been in a motorcycle accident. I was able to minister to him, and now, interestingly, that young man is one of our staff pastors.

Another criticism, harder to accept, came from a woman who apparently wanted more authority in the church for herself and her husband. They both had solid Bible knowledge, but some felt she had a negative, critical spirit. Later I learned this was a pattern from previous churches.

She began criticizing the current leadership, saying we needed to be more selective in whom we chose, needed to develop theological and biblical awareness, and to incorporate more Bible studies into our program for elders.

Ironically, even though I had to confront her on her critical spirit, and she and her husband eventually left the church (which I felt badly about because I loved and respected them), we did recognize some of her observations as valid. There's always a need for more Bible knowledge among leaders. We are now in the process of planning more in-depth Bible study and training for our leaders.

Finally, an organizational example. At elders' meetings, I was passing out the agenda and items to consider at the beginning of the meeting. We interacted well, but one of the elders said, "I think we could better evaluate this material if we could read it and think about it ahead of time. Could you send us the materials and financial reports a few days earlier?"

It was an excellent idea, even though it put pressure on me to get the material together a week earlier. It has cut the time of our meetings in half. The rest of the time we now spend praying for people.

I've discovered I'm not always a detail person — a common problem for many people-oriented leaders. So I've learned to accept suggestions and criticisms that help me in these practical areas especially.

As a whole, how has your leadership style changed since your early days in the first Fellowship Bible Church?

I've gained more self-awareness, more self-honesty, if I may coin that word. If you had asked me ten years ago, "What makes this church work?" I would have said, "Humanly speaking, it's our multiple leadership, primarily the elders."

Today I'd answer that question by saying, "Our elders are key, but I'm the key to helping the elders function." I don't mean to sound egotistical, but I'm more aware of the role I have to play behind the scenes — communicating, motivating, phoning every elder who misses a meeting to fill him in on what happened.

My style is the same as before — laid back but working like crazy. The difference is now I'm willing to admit I'm leading. In the early days I overreacted to authoritarian leadership styles — which I still think are unfortunate — but I've always led. Now I feel I'm more honest with myself and others about the importance of being a strong leader, particularly in a growing church, and yet also developing a strong multiple leadership that does lead as a team.

To whom do you consider yourself accountable? The church elders? The congregation? God alone?

With our multiple-leadership structure, I work closely with our elders at three levels:

First, I'm accountable to them. They have final responsibility to make sure I'm fulfilling my role as senior pastor. This includes making sure my character reflects the qualifications outlined in 1 Timothy 3 and Titus 1. They are my overseers.

Second, as elder/pastor myself, I work with them as "one among equals" in the decision-making process. I bring recommendations and proposals from the staff, but final decisions are made by the group as a whole. Our goal is to reach unity, but I submit to the group's direction.

Third, as senior pastor, my task is to shepherd the elders — to minister in a special way to them and their families on an individual basis.

In addition, I'm responsible, under the direction of the elders, to manage the church staff, to give forthright reports on staff performance and functions — in essence, to act as an "executive officer" who reports to the board. They have the final authority to guide me, correct me, and if need be, remove me from my position should I fail to function as a competent spiritual leader.

What kinds of self-monitoring do you do? Have you seen any self-improvement in your ministry?

One of the tools I use is the Style of Influence test (SOI). This test has helped me tremendously in evaluating my strengths as well as weaknesses.

I think one of the areas I have improved the most is the organization of my messages. As a professor in a classroom — which I was for twenty years — you can depart from your notes, and students don't mind.

Realistically, on how many areas can a pastor concentrate? Not many people can do everything well. How do you narrow your focus to those areas of greatest importance?

For me, the key is remembering my basic priority is to equip the saints to do the work of ministry.

Which includes teaching, preaching, counseling, administration, modeling an evangelistic lifestyle . . . almost everything pastors do can be called "equipping."

Yes, but not in equal measure. I remember writing my first job description when I was teaching a course in administration at Dallas Seminary. I included everything, and when I was done, I had to go back and cross out about three pages, because there was no way I could do it all.

In a church, I have to keep asking, *What will best help me to equip individuals to do the work of ministry?* Of all the things the church needs right now, some are more crucial than others.

When you were sole pastor at the first Fellowship Bible Church, what did you decide you had to focus on, and what were you able to push aside as secondary tasks?

That was a unique situation, because I had two full-time jobs — professor and pastor. As a result, my commitment to the church was to see the ministry done through lay leaders shepherding small groups. That took the bulk of the counseling and ministry of encouragement.

I spent my time preparing my messages and meeting regularly with the elders to encourage the discipling process.

As you evaluate your ministry, is there a time to admit you've done as much as you can, and you should leave that church?

I talked with a young pastor in a rigid independent church not long ago. He's committed to some of the same basics I am: freedom in form but adherence to biblical principles. One of his goals is to equip parents to turn their home into a learning center where children can be nurtured in the faith.

When he presented his plan to the board, one of them said, "I think it's the height of hypocrisy to try turning our homes into learning centers when you and your wife left your kids with a baby sitter so the two of you could take a vacation alone. I'll have you know my wife and I never left our children home on any of our vacations." About half of the other board members agreed.

Facing that kind of rigid mentality, the pastor decided, and I agreed, that it was time for him to move on. He'd brought the church as far as he could, it wasn't going to go much farther, and that kind of abuse is too painful to endure.

It's sad, because the church is losing an excellent pastor. I'm now in the process of trying to help him relocate.

Another time to move is when, for one reason or another, you've lost the respect of the congregation and can't seem to regain it. Then it's better to start fresh somewhere else.

So the principle is learning to recognize when you've gone as far as you're probably going to go — whether it's because of inertia, board disapproval, lack of respect, or whatever. What clues tell you you're reaching that point?

Consistent resistance. Especially if you've taken all the

steps to resolve conflict — asking if you've offended anyone or if you're moving too fast, negotiating, apologizing if necessary.

I was in one ministry (not a church) where I kept pushing for a particular program, and it kept getting shot down. I kept working at it but couldn't get a hearing. It was as if the powers that be were saying, "Getz has gotten his way on just about everything he's gone after, and he's not going to get this one."

I eventually left, and the next thing I knew, my successor got the program I had been pushing for.

If the pastors you know were to evaluate themselves, what strengths would they find?

I would say a commitment to the Word of God and a belief that the Word of God can change people's lives. Most pastors I know and minister to through the Center for Church Renewal really desire to do God's will and trust in his power for the results.

S E V E N

GRASPING THE VISION

Vision arises out of our burden to know the will of God, to become whatever it is God wants us to become.

EVERETT "TERRY" FULLAM

Everett "Terry" Fullam

In a corner of Terry Fullam's office sits an architect's model of a large sanctuary, gathering dust. It is a silent reminder that visions do not always become reality.

"That's what we thought God wanted us to build five or six years ago, when our present building was first filled up," the bespectacled rector recalls with a grin. "The place was packed; we were having four morning services — time to build a bigger barn. It was going to go right out on the front lawn. The vestry and congregation were all unanimous.

"But when we went to the city fathers for approval, they were just as unanimous: NO. Our plans would be a massive overdevelopment of this wooded area, they ruled."

Only then, says Fullam, was the church ready to comprehend an alternate vision. It came as a message from the church's senior warden: "God wants us instead to build the living church, to give ourselves to strengthening his people, not only here in Darien, but across the nation and even the world."

That is what has happened. Saint Paul's Episcopal Church has become a hive of renewal throughout the Connecticut suburbs of New York City and beyond, with thirteen hundred worshipers coming to the four weekly services, two of which are held in a high school auditorium. Four times a year, pastors and church leaders trek to Saint Paul's for clergy conferences; in between times, Terry Fullam spends major amounts of time on the road, speaking mainly to ministerial groups.

It's fitting that a section on the leader's tasks begin with a discussion of vision, and it's just as fitting that the interview be with a man who has been a realistic visionary in a local church come alive.

Who originates the vision for a church — God, humans, or both?

Vision is the product of God working in us. He creates the vision, and we receive it; it becomes a rallying point, a goal toward which we move as his people. Without it, as the Scripture says, "the people perish."

In my own case, the Lord spent most of a summer working on me to prepare me for this church, first through Scripture and then through a rather strange experience that is, I suppose, unique to me. I had been a college professor up until then, so it took a lot of extra effort to implant the vision of the parish ministry in me.

I didn't hear God audibly, but his word to me was so clear that, had I heard him out loud, it would have added nothing. It gave me the courage to step into an unfamiliar role. It has provided a stability for me ever since.

What were the specifics?

I was on a study tour in the Holy Land. Two days before leaving the United States, I had received a call from the vestry of this church. I was very reluctant.

Then I noticed one morning in 2 Chronicles 15 a mention about Israel's decline for lack of "a teaching priest." I knew all about teaching, of course, and I was familiar with the priesthood, but could the two be combined? Apparently so.

Later I was deeply challenged by Jeremiah 23, which described "prophets who prophesy to you, filling you with vain hopes; they speak visions of their own minds, not from the mouth of the Lord. . . . But if they had stood in my council, then they would have proclaimed my words to my people, and they would have turned them from their evil way, and from the evil of their doings" (vv. 16, 22).

Then came the moment in the middle of the night, while in the Sinai, that God put the pieces together by saying, "You are to go to that church, for I have chosen that congregation to do a mighty work for my name's sake." He went on to reveal what the church could become. I was astounded.

How did this personal vision of ministry affect your beginnings there?

When I stepped into the pulpit here on October 1, 1972 — my first Sunday — I said to those 175 people, "One of two things will happen to you over the next months and years. Either you will find yourself opening up more and more to the Lord, in which case you will sense you are growing spiritually. Or else you will find yourself tightening up, constricting, to the point the atmosphere will become intolerable."

That was a strong thing to say — but it proved true. I went on to make a promise: "When I stand in this pulpit, I want you to know that at least *I* think God has given me something to say. And I make a covenant with you: If he doesn't speak, I won't." This deep conviction had been born out of Jeremiah 23.

Did God ever call your bluff?

Yes! The second Sunday of January 1973 found me absolutely blank. I had gone though my usual discipline of sermon preparation and come up empty. Not that I couldn't stand up and talk in a reasonably meaningful way about Scripture — I had done that in the classroom for years. But this particular week, I had not heard from God.

It got to be Saturday. Finally it was evening. I still had nothing at all. I went over the next day's lections again. Still nothing.

I went back to the church late that night to pray. "Lord, are you testing me on what I said? If so, I really meant it. I'm perfectly willing to go to the congregation tomorrow morning and say, 'There won't be any sermon today.' "

Still no quickening in my spirit. Nothing.

The next morning, the worship service began. It came time for me to preach. I was literally on my way to the pulpit, preparing to make my embarrassing announcement, when suddenly it flashed in my mind that I should tell the Sinai experience. I had not thought about that once the whole previous week.

So I told the story. I know now that the Lord did this on purpose. If he had instructed me ahead of time, I would have disobeyed, for all kinds of reasons. Nothing about this church seemed ready for such a tale. I told not only what had happened to me but also what God had said about this church and what he intended to do with it. I told how the voice inside my head had said, "I want to move in a powerful way in that church. It will not be like other churches. Don't put your eyes upon another church and try to copy its program. That is not my plan. . . . I'm going to change the congregation, from altar to window and wall to wall." The whole vision was spilled — when none of it had even begun to take shape!

It's now been well over a decade since, and the Lord has been filling in the parts and pieces. People still remember that Sunday and talk about it occasionally. From that day on, of course, I was free to share the vision from time to time, keeping it before the people.

Bob Slosser's book *Miracle at Darien* tells how you made quite a point at the beginning of saying, "I will not be the head of this church. Christ is the Head, and we must take our directions from him." How does a statement like that become more than rhetoric?

We stumbled onto that before I had been rector here forty-eight hours. At a special meeting of the vestry on Monday night, October 2, I began by reading some Scripture about the church as the body of Christ, and Jesus as the Head. That led me to pose some questions to the people sitting around the table.

I'd always believed the theology, of course, but not once in my life had I ever applied it to church governance. I was an American, with a built-in bias toward things democratic. The way to guide a group was to do what most of them wanted.

But I asked that night, "If Jesus is the Head of the church, and if it's the function of a head to direct the body, then doesn't that mean he is supposed to direct us?"

Well, yes, that was the implication, they said.

"So, if he is leading and we're listening," I continued, "is it conceivable that he would lead, say, ten people one way and two another?"

"No," they said, "if he's leading us, he would lead us together."

Inadvertently, we had stumbled upon a second principle: that we could move in the unity of the Spirit. We weren't looking for unity. We were looking for how to function under the headship of Christ, and we stumbled onto unity.

The whole vestry embraced the concept that night — a miracle. Some of the members at that point were not even believing people, and yet they agreed that if this was the way God meant the church to be, that's how we would function. We committed ourselves to think of the church principally as an organism, not so much as an organization.

Some would say that such a view, while noble in intent, gives the veto to the most irascible or ornery member of the group. Any one person can stymie the vision.

That is true. But in practice, it doesn't work that way. The group is so intent on finding the mind of God that unity emerges. Hundreds of churches across the nation are coming to experience this.

I know of one church where a board member had always voted against the others. That was his chosen role — to obstruct. The others came to an understanding of Christ as the Head of the church and decided they would stop overruling this fellow as they had always done in the past. They went through three monthly meetings without passing a single action, because the direction of the Head was not unanimously perceived.

Near the end of the third meeting, the man began to sob. He confessed that all his life he'd taken the opposing point of view; it was the only way to be noticed. He hadn't really expected anyone to do anything about it. At that point, his heart was changed.

If the heart of the people is to find the will of God, I don't think God will allow this kind of vetoing to go on indefinitely. My counsel is: Don't ignore the obstructionist. If God can speak through Balaam's ass, he can speak through any designated leader in the church. In fact, part of what you want to convey is that he or she is part of this chain of communication. Trust the process; watch God work it out.

We have taken the position that *no* vestry person knows what God's will is until we all know.

Do you think average church members care all that much about a church's vision, so long as their particular interests are addressed?

It tends to come to the fore in churches that are open to the Lord and concerned with finding his purposes for individual and corporate life. The notion of vision requires some kind of personal encounter with Christ. If church is mainly a matter of ritual and ceremony, the subject of vision doesn't come up very often.

Is there a difference between vision and goal setting, other than that one sounds spiritual and the other businesslike?

Yes. Vision arises out of our burden to know the will of God, to become whatever it is God wants us to become. Goal setting is a projection of our perceptions of what we want to accomplish. There's nothing particularly nefarious about that. It's just that vision is something that elicits a response from us, that calls us forth. Goals, on the other hand, are things *we* project.

That is why I suppose I'm not firmly committed to goals — I (or we) thought them up in the first place. Vision, on the other hand, *summons* me.

Again the process of goal setting cannot be bad. But if the church is indeed an organism and I am part of the body of Christ, it's not really a matter of "Where do I want to go?" but rather "Where does he want to take me?"

So then perhaps goals come after vision?

I think so. Here at Saint Paul's, we have set intermediate

goals along the way to achieve the vision. I had a clear word from the Lord in the beginning that I was never to regard this as "my church." He was only asking me for obedience as he brought about what he wanted; in other words, he really did intend to build his own church. What was *not* given to me in that vision, however, were the steps by which this was to be achieved.

What are some of your goals here that emerge from the overall vision?

One would be to evangelize every member. We have a saying in the Episcopal church that we have sacramentalized our people but not evangelized them. We have done everything to them you can: we've baptized them, confirmed them, and all the rest, but we need to make sure we introduce them to a personal faith in Jesus Christ.

This is important for two reasons: The Lord wants us to do it, and the church will be strong only to the degree that people are committed to Christ.

So in pursuing this goal, we make an interesting assumption: we assume a person does *not* have a relationship with Jesus Christ unless he is prepared to say he does. The simple fact of being in the church is not enough. We don't argue with people; we don't sit in judgment on their salvation; but neither do we take it for granted that they have committed their lives to Christ unless they say so.

This obviously affects the way we go about many things in the church.

Second, in the case of believers — and this will seem like the exact opposite — we assume commitment rather than noncommitment. I'll give an example. We have a number of clergy and lay leadership conferences here every year, drawing people from all over the world. And we house them in the homes of the parish. For many years, I used to go to the congregation and say, 'A conference is coming up, and we need two hundred beds; please sign up." We always got what we needed, but it was a hassle.

Then one day, I realized all that wasn't necessary. I went

before the congregation one Sunday and said, "You have all heard me ask for beds for the last time. From now on, we will assume that if you have an extra bed in your house, of course you would let someone use it. Because everything you have belongs to the Lord and you've consecrated your home to his service, naturally you would make it available to his servants. So we have made up a bed bank for the parish, and we'll assume yours are available. If for some reason you cannot host a guest, you let us know. Otherwise, we will assume commitment rather than noncommitment." The people readily agreed that that was the way to look at it.

So many clergy pitch the level of their ministry to the least committed members of the congregation, being careful not to offend them. That's not what we were called to do.

You've been here more than a dozen years. What is there yet to do? Do you want to build a larger building so you don't have to keep meeting at the high school?

That would be fine. Our present arrangements are not adequate. I suppose when the Lord thinks he can trust us, he'll let us have a building. But that has never been part of the vision. We've been busy building the living church, so that over half the giving here goes into mission beyond the borders of Saint Paul's. If we were building a building, we might have to cut back on that.

But there's much more to be done. We need to find more effective ways to equip the saints for ministry. We already have a lot of instruction going on at various levels, but I'm thinking about several outstanding people who are coming up to early retirement. I feel a great sense of stewardship for such magnificent gifts, to help them discern the ministry God has called them to.

Another task is to influence the wider church toward better preparation for ordination. There has to be a better way than most of our current models. Perhaps Saint Paul's can be a "teaching parish" to show the way.

Then, we're just novices when it comes to *pastoring* the body of Christ here. I'm not thinking of crisis intervention so much as nurturing people through the plateaus and rough spots in their lives. The necessary gifts are resident in the church; we just have to put them together with the needs.

What are the impediments to these visions?

Like any group of church leaders, we face the need for constant "deprogramming." My vestry members come from long days in the business offices of New York City and the surrounding area, and they struggle to get to the point of being able to hear the Lord speak. We've talked about that a lot together. My task is to help them focus, to remind them we're a body of people God is preparing to use. We also have to remind ourselves constantly what we're about. We're not here to negotiate — "I'll give in on this if you'll give in on that." Rather, we're actively seeking the mind of the Lord, and we believe the Lord will speak to us *corporately*, not individually. He never seems to give the whole vision to any one of us. We're constantly putting together a jigsaw puzzle.

There's a great difference between our vestry and a board of directors. In the early days, we had the conventional approach of each member being responsible for some area of church life. We found that to be an unnecessary layer of authority, since most of the ministries were being done by people who knew much more about them than the vestry.

Now we seek to be a group that discerns the Lord's direction, the vision seekers. And I'm willing, as rector, to tie myself to the common vision received by the whole of the board in unity.

Isn't that a risky statement?

I made it when I came, and I've never regretted it. As I look back, I can think of no vestry decision I would have disagreed with. If the group seeks God's will and comes to a sense of peace, I'm satisfied.

How does this work at the congregational level, where you have many more people and vastly differing levels of spiritual maturity? Can you get unity there?

76385

The unity need only be as broad as the group having the authority. In the Episcopal church, the congregation holds relatively little authority. They elect officers — and in this particular church, they also vote on the choice of a new rector.

But on those matters, yes — we have moved only in unity. Our selection process of nomination and voting is like many other churches, I suppose, but throughout the whole search each fall for four new vestry members is this assumption: God has four people to fill those positions, and we must find them. After careful prayer and discussion at several levels, four names are presented. We've never had a negative vote.

If we did, it wouldn't be any scandal. We would simply withdraw that person's name and start all over, until we were sure we had found God's choice.

Please understand: Our goal is not to maintain unity. Our goal is to move under the headship of Christ. Unity is simply the gift he gives us when we find his mind.

Have you at times been frustrated waiting for unity to come?

Not really. I remember the time we wanted to sponsor a Vietnamese refugee family, and all but one vestryman were in favor of it. A committee had done all the studying and planning, and here was this one holdout. He felt we weren't paying enough attention to material needs in our own membership.

We didn't press; I didn't try to coerce. We brought the subject up again the next month and found we were at the same place as before. We tabled the subject again.

At the third meeting, the man said, "You know, I'm so embarrassed, but now at last I have a sense of peace about bringing this family. Let's move ahead."

It was only then that we learned the family didn't want the Connecticut climate and had settled instead in a warmer state. Had we moved earlier, we might have caused them considerable unhappiness.

We then proceeded — unanimously — to set up a cash assistance program to help those in the parish with financial needs. We learned something here about "the fullness of time." We learned that you can trust the process. So what if it takes a while longer? It's all right. Something unseen may be working itself out.

Do you follow any pattern or regimen in defining vision or setting goals?

I have to rearticluate the vision every time we bring new communicants into the fellowship. I usually address the issue also on a Sunday morning around the anniversary of my coming here.

The vestry spends time on these things regularly. We go on retreats; we're constantly talking about what the needs are, what has been slipping through the cracks, what the Lord might be saying to us about various concerns.

How can a vision be propagated, besides through preaching?

Teaching and preaching are the principal formats, but there's also the prophetic function — interpreting where God is already at work. That is part of comprehending vision.

I did something last Sunday in this area. It was the Feast of Christ the King, the last Sunday of the church year, just before Advent. I talked about how Christmas doesn't make sense without Easter, and Easter doesn't make sense without this day, the revelation of Jesus as Lord. If he is Lord, I said, he holds rights to all the gifts he has given us. I then asked every communicant of the church to take stock of his or her life and write me a letter. "This is a large parish," I said, "and I'm unable to be with each of you individually. But I want to be alongside you in prayer.

"You know that I pray through the parish list on a regular basis. So look at the stewardship of your life — your natural abilities and your opportunities — and tell me in letter form about yourself. What obedience is the Lord calling you to? What thing is he commending? What are your dreams for your life, for this body, and for the interplay between the two?"

I told them I would pray for each of them. I announced that on Christmas Eve I would bring all the letters to the altar, offering their gifts to the Lord. And then at this time next year, I will mail all the letters back for review.

There's a great reservoir of commitment in this church and a desire to find God's will. In this way, I hope to help people focus on vision.

Give some examples of churches you know and their specific callings.

The Church of the Redeemer in Houston has had a great ministry in music. Their tapes and records have gone all over the world for years.

College Hill Presbyterian Church in Cincinnati has an outstanding lay pastoral ministry. It's a model for other churches.

Saint Luke's Episcopal in Bath, Ohio — a small community — is a powerful church. People go there from all over to learn about youth ministry, sometimes staying for up to three months and paying tuition for the training they receive.

Saint Andrew's by the Sea in Destin, Florida, a little fishing town, draws people from all around to its counseling ministry.

Each of these has other ministries as well, of course, but I've singled out their special contribution to the church at large.

You didn't become an Episcopalian until around age thirty. You were raised in Baptist and Congregational churches, served on the pastoral staff of Tremont Temple in Boston, and taught at Barrington College. What did you learn about vision in these various settings?

My vision of the church today is of three streams leading into one river. From the historic Protestant side comes the emphasis on the Word, the priesthood of the believer, and the need for individual, personal encounter with God. From the Catholic stream comes the idea of the corporate body of Christ — that you can't be a Christian all by yourself. Then the third stream is the charismatic dimension, which emphasizes the immediacy of God's working in our lives. The operation of the Spirit does not supplant the Scripture in any way, but it shows that God still speaks to us today, through prophecy and in other ways as well.

So my personal quest is for wholeness, for moving from a partial to a more adequate understanding of the vision, both personal and corporate. The church as I see it needs to be Catholic, Protestant, and charismatic all at once.

As you travel and spend time with pastors and church leaders, what do you observe about their vision?

Many of them are very discouraged. They have tried everything they know to do, without much response. Some say to me, "I haven't found the ministry fulfilling at all; it's horrendous, and I'd get out of it if I could, but I'm not trained to do anything else."

This kind of malaise is partly because for so long the church has been bereft of any significant biblical preaching and teaching. These languishing leaders are themselves products of a "professional" ministry. They are sincere, but they haven't caught any kind of vision from the Lord, and so they resort to human methods to try to get the job done.

One man came to a conference here from a church in Fairfield, Alabama, to which the bishop had sent him with the instructions, "Close the place, and I'll be happy with you; it hasn't done anything in a hundred years." He couldn't quite bring himself to do that, but he was so frustrated, he was ready to leave the ministry.

He listened to the preaching and teaching in the conference, and he began to catch a vision. He went back to Alabama and said, "Lord, I suppose I always knew you were the Head of the church, but I must have forgotten it. I've tried everything I know in this place, and it's gone nowhere. But now, I want to promise you that I will do whatever it takes to establish your headship over this church in a functional way, even if it means I have to pump gas for a living."

That degree of commitment brought astonishing results. Today that congregation is a leader in the South. Blacks and whites are worshiping together there and redeeming whole neighborhoods as they move to be close to the church. They've had to build a larger building. The vision has taken hold and is being perpetuated.

For a lot of clergy, their vision is essentially limited to the expectations of the people around them. No wonder they get bogged down. Our vision must not be confined to our circumstances, or it will be forever small. It must instead be a vision engendered by the Scripture and supported by the Spirit.

E I G H T

SETTING PRIORITIES

One of the biggest mistakes that can be made at a planning session is to directly or indirectly say to our leaders, "What can you do to help me pull off my objectives?"

HOWARD HENDRICKS

Howard Hendricks

Visions, as compelling as they are, are not enough. It is one thing to know what this church can be; it is another thing, and far more difficult, to know how to get there. Leaders wrestle with pressing practicalities: What do we tackle first? And second? Can we afford to leave anything for later? With so much to be done, and every contemplated action a good one, how do we sort the good from the very good from the best? What is truly essential?

Offering insight on these questions is Howard Hendricks, a nationally recognized Christian educator. After ministering in a number of local churches, he joined the faculty of Dallas Theological Seminary, where he has served for the last thirty-six years. He is chairman of the Center for Christian Leadership, is in constant demand for clergy and lay conferences, and is heard daily on a syndicated radio program, "The Art of Family Living." Dr. Hendricks is the author of three books, including Heaven Help the Home! (Victor).

In this interview you'll see the practical suggestions, radiant good will, and relaxed humor that have made Howard Hendricks beloved by students and colleagues alike.

If you were to call the church staff and/or lay leaders together for a planning retreat, what questions would you want the group to discuss before launching another year of ministry?

At the beginning of any new ministry year, a church must evaluate its past performance. I would use three questions:

1. "What are we doing well? What are our strengths?" If you don't capitalize on your strengths, you tend to minister on the basis of weaknesses.

2. "What are we doing that needs to be improved?" You may be doing many things reasonably well, but how much can you improve them? We are embarrassed by our weaknesses and we excuse them rather than find ways to overcome them.

3. "What are we not doing that we should be doing?" Many churches tend to do what any other human organization can do, instead of what the church alone can do. In planning a new church year, church leaders must be aware of the unique contribution the church makes to the community — the spiritual contribution.

Give us an example of a church that has a particular strength and has built upon it.

The First Evangelical Free Church in Fullerton, California, is a classic example of a church that knows its primary strength — in this case, expository preaching and teaching. Because this is understood, the pastor, Chuck Swindoll, is released to do what he is eminently gifted to do. You have to stand in line to get a seat.

On the other hand, I was in a church some time ago that has an unusual strength in fellowship. I was so impressed I said to the pastor, "How do you attract this many friendly couples to one church?"

He said, "It's simple. You can't get in and out of this church without somebody inviting you to lunch."

Even though it's massive, it's the friendliest church on planet Earth, with a fellowship virus that has spread to everyone. Objectively, I wouldn't say it was the greatest preaching center in the area, but it's developed this one strength to an inspiring level.

Isn't there a danger of emphasizing one strength to the exclusion of others?

Yes, that's the other side of the coin. You can go overboard in emphasizing your strengths and neglect the many other necessary ministries that make up a church. A pastor needs a broad perspective. He is not the pastor of any segment in the church; he is the pastor of the total church — cradle roll, children, youth, adults, and senior citizens. One pastor can't personally minister to all of these groups, but he can develop a leader for each church ministry. The pastor's job is the big picture — the ministry vision.

Can you isolate the points of strength that should exist in any size church for it to be balanced, healthy, and dynamic?

Chapter two of Acts gives the heart of a New Testament church. In this context four essential disciplines stand out:

Instruction. The church that ceases to educate ceases to exist. "They continued steadfastly in the apostles' teaching."

Worship. Worship is the by-product of instruction. It is impossible to worship a God you don't know. Worship is a personal response to a divine revelation. And by response, I don't mean shaking the pastor's hand at the door and saying, "That was a wonderful sermon." Real response answers the question, "What am I going to do about divine revelation?"

Service. The New Testament believers became involved in the needs of the body. Service may take a variety of forms, but it always comes out of worship. People say to me, "What we need in our church is more workers."

I say, "No, you don't need more workers; you need more worshipers." I've never seen a worshiper who didn't go to work, but there are a lot of people busy at some kind of religious work who have never worshiped. They are working in the energy of the flesh rather than in the power of the Spirit.

Fellowship. "They continued steadfastly in the apostles' fellowship" — which to us is coffee and donuts. How in the world did the early church have fellowship without coffee and donuts? They had something better; they had persecution. There is no greater fellowship than being involved in the person and work of Jesus Christ while under duress.

Now the context of the paragraph at the end of this chapter is evangelism. It begins with people being added to the church daily, and it ends the same way. If the church ever loses its evangelistic thrust in the process of teaching, worshiping, serving, and fellowshiping, these disciplines will degenerate into ends, rather than means to an end.

What can pastors do to help their leaders set priorities with attention to these four areas?

One of the biggest mistakes that can be made at a planning session is to directly or indirectly say to our leaders, "What can you do to help me pull off my objectives?" These people are more than elders or staff members; they're parents, spouses, business people, members of the community. Until we start ministering at that level, we are going to focus upon what they do rather than who they are.

The key is to care about people as people. One of our leading Dallas businessmen came in to see me the other day and said, "You know, everybody and his brother wants my money, and I'm delighted to invest it in the Lord's work, but doesn't anybody know that I have needs?"

But how can a pastor pay attention to instruction, worship, service, and fellowship, and also give this kind of personal attention? Isn't it more than the pastor can do?

The pastor can't do all this. The pastor-teacher's primary task is to be an equipper of the saints for their work of ministry. He's committed to a ministry of multiplication, not addition. He's not doing the work of ten, he's equipping ten to do the work.

Many of our board members aren't involved in spiritual ministry; they're involved in activities that others in the congregation can do. If a Christian leader is going to make a spiritual impact, he must surround himself with a group of people into whose lives he's pouring his own — which, by the way, is a tremendous blessing to him.

I spend an incredible amount of time with students, but I don't do a lot of other things. You can't do everything. I can't write all of the books I would like to write. I can't go to all the places I would like to go if I'm going to build something lasting into the lives of my students.

Describe instruction, the first discipline you mentioned.

We have the idea that instruction has to take place within four walls. They might be one of the greatest barriers to learning. For example, I can teach for hours in a classroom, walk down to the snack shop, sit down with a student, and get involved in a conversation that will change his life. That doesn't mean I should abandon classroom teaching, but some of my most effective teaching has been done in my office, over at the snack shop, and out at my home.

I told Dr. Walvoord once, "I don't know why you pay me, because I don't really do that much in class. I do most of my work outside of class."

He said, "Well, we could solve that problem." *(Laughter)*

So as church leaders establish priorities, they need to ask themselves about the degree to which they are discipling others.

Discipleship can be a fad. Wherever I go, I discover it's the "in" term. But where are the results? It doesn't make any difference if you change the label on an empty bottle. True discipleship is a commitment, a lifestyle.

One of the questions I ask a pastor — I love to do it particularly when I'm leaving — is, "When I come back, I am going to ask you to show me the core of people whose lives you are building. Who will be here when you are gone?" The answer comes from effective preaching and discipling.

One day at a pastors' conference my subject was, "Have

You Never Read Ephesians 4?" I said, "You say, 'Of couse I've read it. I've preached on it.' Jesus Christ said eleven different times to the most well-read people of his time, 'Have you never read?' Of course they had read; they spent most of their life reading, but they didn't apply what they read."

When I finished, a little old man sitting up front came to me, tears of joy pouring down his face, and said, "Sir, I want you to know that I have spent thirty-nine years doing the work of the ministry, and three years equipping saints for their work of ministry. I'd like you to know I've accomplished more in the last three years than the first thirty-nine."

Suppose a pastor says, "I'd like to instruct the saints to do the work of ministry, but I'm not sure how to start."

How did Jesus Christ train his men? The Lord Jesus sent his disciples out after he had carefully instructed them in how to minister. When they came back they were higher than a kite. The text says they rehearsed everything that had happened. And he was excited with them.

On another occasion they went out on their own and struck out. Jesus bailed them out, performed the miracle they had blown, and the text says, "The disciples took him aside and privately asked, 'What happened?' He said, 'This kind comes out by prayer only.' " Prayer? What in the world does prayer have to do with it? You see, they had cast out demons before and they had done it successfully. Now they were learning they had been spending too much time using their gift and not enough time developing the spiritual resources to maximize their gift.

Based on those accounts, what specific things would you do to equip your leaders?

I'd do a number of things. I'd start a Bible study that revolved around passages such as Acts 2, Ephesians 4, and Matthew 28, and get them involved in a discovery process. We tell people too much and don't let them discover things for themselves. We don't hear an "Aha!" often enough.

I'll never forget one time when I was studying a passage of Scripture with a group of men, and one of them said, "Hey, hold it! I've got the picture! Jesus Christ never became blind to his objectives. He was always on target!"

I said, "Okay, why don't we come up with our objectives?" The next time we met they came with their lists. We lined them up, and I said, "You prioritize them." For the first time, some of them began to focus the gospel upon their daily lives.

One man quietly said, "It's hard for me to believe this, but something that's number two in my priority list is number twenty-two in my life." The impact upon his life of that confession was twice as great because *he* had discovered it.

We need to spend more time in our retreat and board meetings praying, studying, and sharing. I was meeting with a church board one night when it really got heavy. Finally the pastor broke down; I mean he broke down and wept like a baby. In between sobs he said, "Men, I just can't carry this load."

Then one member said, "This isn't your burden; this is ours." That launched a discussion that went until midnight about our ministry responsibilities as lay leaders.

Worship was the second discipline. You said instruction leads to worship. How?

Worship is a personal response to a divine revelation. You haven't worshiped until you've responded.

I had an elder who would have failed an audition for a deaf choir, but during the hymns he would stand down in front of me with a hymnbook open, mouthing the words. One day I said to him, "Mr. McFadden, what are you doing?"

He said, "I'm worshiping."

I asked, "You mean you're repeating the words?"

He replied, "That's right. Remember, Pastor, you haven't worshiped until you've told God your personal response."

As long as people continue going out of our churches saying, "My, that was a wonderful sermon," they will know nothing of worship. When a person meets you at the door and says, "Pastor, isn't he a wonderful Lord?" you'd better shout "Glory!" because you might have met one worshiper.

How can we prepare people for what should happen on Sunday morning?

I happen to have the crazy idea that preaching should precede rather than follow the worship service. Preaching should be followed by sharing, application, prayer, and other worship responses, and that requires careful planning and training.

We should prepare our people for change. Individually, we are predestined to be changed, conformed to the image of Jesus Christ. Corporately, the church should be the most revolutionary agency on earth, and yet it is often set in concrete. People come unglued because the service didn't start with the Gloria Patri, or the Lord's Prayer was in the wrong place. Board members, who are the opinion shapers, must set the worship pace and say to the people: "This is what we are going to do and this is why we are going to do it."

What should church leaders consider when discussing the discipline of service?

I see service as what goes on in the office or factory Monday through Friday. The average layperson has the idea that his vocation is his penalty. That's what he does five days a week in order to "serve the Lord" on Sunday. Actually, what takes place on Sunday should equip him for the service he's going to perform all week.

We also need to recognize that within the church many of our people are overworked and undertrained. I find more and more people who do not enjoy church work — they endure it. My goal for a local church would be to help every member serve Christ, in at least one way, outside as well as inside the church. The average lay person isn't serving in that way because he's not trained to do it; but once he's properly trained, it's amazing how he will begin to enjoy it and become comfortable with it. How you enlist a person usually determines how he or she will serve. A moratorium should be declared on at least three ways of enlisting people. One is the public announcement read on Sunday morning: "Beloved, next Tuesday we are going visiting. Please show up. Last week nobody showed up. Won't you please come this week?" Usually, no one will come the following week except the two people you should never send visiting!

Another one is last-minute conscription; it's the situation where the Sunday school superintendent slips in during the adult class opening exercises, taps the person on the end of the row, and sentences him to the junior department for life. The moral of which is, "Don't sit on the end of the row."

The third scene is a desperate C. E. director who approaches a sincere, goodhearted person and says, "We've been all over the building looking for someone to take the high school class and we can't find anybody who wants to take it. We've lost six people in the last seven months, and now we're coming to you. Will you take it?" If this goodhearted Christian says, "Well, I don't have much time," the C. E. director usually responds, "That's all right. It won't take much time."

It has always fascinated me that when we take people into a local church — the time of their greatest motivation, namely, their willingness to unite with the church — we tell them to sit down, keep quiet, and listen. After we have made spectators of them, we try to reverse their orientation to one of participation. The time to give members some responsibility is when they join the church. People need to know we're not operating the Church of the Sacred Rest.

Would you go so far as to say that everybody in the church must have a place of service?
Precisely.

Have you ever seen a church like that?
No, but I've seen one close to it. I saw a church go from about 34 percent participation, which is high, to 93 percent. They committed themselves to the idea that everyone in the

church was going to have a responsibility. No exceptions. They matched person with job and began to develop a realistic training program.

What is a realistic training program?

A good combination of input and involvement, a hands-on type of thing. Learn to teach by teaching. I've never heard of a correspondence course in swimming, yet this is similar to the methodology we use in trying to prepare people for service. I like the idea of apprenticeship. If you develop workers with the idea of long-term commitments, you'll train some real experts. I can give you hundreds of illustrations.

For instance, the greatest nursery teacher I know is a person who has been teaching for thirty-eight years. If there is anything to be known about teaching nursery children, she knows it. Even more exciting, she's trained another twenty-five or thirty people in her skills. I've heard her say, "I'm no good with adults; they threaten me." But she loves little kids and they love her.

How do you reshape the thinking of those members who have already developed "spectatoritis"?

In a number of ways. Many churches have used questionnaires effectively — a means by which people can indicate the service areas that interest them. There is one warning I give to churches using surveys: Follow through! I recently had lunch with some upset people who had filled out an interest survey last winter, expressed interest in several areas of service, and were still waiting to hear from the church. It will be a cold August day in Dallas before they sign up for something again.

How you follow through is important. I recommend that a committee examine the data, match the jobs with available people, and — this is the key — go to the prospect personally and say, "The committee has spent a lot of time thinking and praying about the matter, and we feel that God would have us approach you about the possibility of working in such-and-such a position."

We enlisted a neurosurgeon to serve in our college department in this manner. Three of us made an appointment and went to see him. When he saw us he said, "Good grief, what is this?"

"Well," we said, "we have a challenge for you." Before we could continue, he called his nurse and told her not to disturb him for any reason. We described the task as clearly as we could, and then very straightforwardly told him, "Doc, it will take everything you have and then some, but we think you're our man."

That night he couldn't sleep. His wife asked, "What's the matter?"

He replied, "I have to make an important decision. I'm struggling with the fact that three Spirit-led men came to my office and said, 'We feel that God would have us approach you about the possibility of taking the college class.' How can I view that lightly?"

What's important for church leaders to reexamine about the fourth priority, fellowship?

First of all, we tend to stifle fellowship — which means to share in common — by gravitating toward vertical rather than horizontal relationships: professor and student, teacher and disciple, pastor and parishioner. We need more horizontal relationships that are developed around commitment to the same goals. Regardless of our station in life, all of us are in the process of learning and maturing.

Second, the average lay person doesn't think that his vocation has spiritual importance. Most physicians, salespersons, and business managers think their "secular" tasks are unrelated to the body of Christ. Our faith commitment to each other should be the great equalizer. Because we are members of the same family, it's very important to me, the pastor, for Jim, an elder in our congregation, to do good work at the local television station. I am going to pray for him and support him in his work.

How can a pastor demonstrate this kind of fellowship in a tangible way?

I've asked lay people if their pastor has ever shown up at their job. They usually respond, "Don't kid me." Once I was at Dick Halverson's church, and he said, "How would you like to make a call with me?" We went out to a junior high school where one of Dick's members was the principal. He was expecting us, and had some sandwiches brought up from the cafeteria. After lunch, we studied the Word and spent some time praying together. Just before we left, Dick said, "Let's take a walk." So the three of us walked all the way around the block. After we had returned to the front door, Dick said, "Let's pray and claim this place as your center of ministry." Dick was as concerned about this man's ministry as he was about his own. He sought to help equip him to function as a Christian leader in society. That's how you develop fellowship.

It's easy to forget our spiritual opposition. We can leave a planning meeting without realizing there is a power totally committed to blocking or destroying what God wants us to be and do. Good strategy demands that we size up the enemy forces. How do we do this?

The Devil is a better student of us than we are of him. Paul said in 2 Corinthians that we are not ignorant of his devices. We know how he operates. But that's an admonition few people take seriously.

I'm afraid we have something of a cavalier attitude toward the Devil. The older I become, the more I am aware of the subtlety of Satan. Just when you think you have him figured out, he slips up on your blind side.

When you are doing what Jesus Christ has called you to do, you can count on two things: You will possess spiritual power because you have the presence of Christ, and you'll experience opposition because the Devil does not concentrate on secondary targets. He never majors on the minor.

Neither should we.

N I N E

MAKING DECISIONS

Virtually every decision has a moral aspect, but there are also other modes to consider: effective versus ineffective, good versus best, safe versus risky.

CARL F. GEORGE

Carl F. George

It's not stretching it too far to say a leader is much like a basketball referee: in the middle of the action, trying to keep the game clean and fair, and above all, calling 'em as he sees 'em.

Decision making is just as important and difficult to the pastor as to the ref — and occasionally just as unpopular.

One of the best at making the right call is Carl George. Director of the Pasadena-based Charles E. Fuller Institute of Evangelism and Church Growth since 1978, he spends a full one-third of his time with individual churches and pastors who have requested help. His wisdom is a combination of thirteen years in the pastorate (University Baptist Church, Gainesville, Florida), consulting work with more than three dozen denominations, postgraduate study in sociology, and wide self-education, all processed by one of the fastest minds in the West.

Here are his thoughts on the demanding art of making decisions.

Everyone knows leadership involves making decisions; that's "what we get paid for," as the saying goes. How can church leaders do it better?

As I spend time with pastors, I find them making many decisions every day. But they are handicapped because they almost inevitably think in moralistic terms only: rightness versus wrongness. "What's the *right* thing to do? What *ought* to be done?"

I keep reminding leaders that there are other modes to consider: effective versus ineffective, good versus best, safe versus risky.

You're not dismissing the moral dimension?

Not at all. Virtually every decision has a moral aspect, either in its consequences or in the way the decision will be implemented. And most of us in the ministry carry an intuitive desire to reach for the godly, to hear the words of God on a given issue and line up with him rather than against him. But not all church administration deals with Mount Sinai issues. Many decisions are more mundane and subtle.

That's why I prefer to guide pastors toward such questions as:

— What are the decisions I could make, and what will be the outcomes? Are they significant to my long-term ministry? Which decisions ought to be deferred?

— What are my options? Is this really a yes/no question? Or are there options *A*, *B*, and *C* to be considered?

— Who should be involved in the decision-making process in order for implementation to be effective?

— How do I know when I have enough information? When is going for more research just a way of delaying the decision? Is it time to bite the bullet?

These are the questions that aren't asked often enough.

Of the many decisions pastors face — from "What shall I preach?" to "Whom shall we hire?" to "How shall I arrange

my life to be a good spouse and parent?" — which tend to buffalo pastors the worst?

One of the toughest ones, in my judgment, is what to do with one's time on a daily basis. The trouble with time is that no one holds pastors accountable for it. They can wallow along ineffectively day after day, their actions not really adding up to anything in particular, and no one notices.

How do *you* notice, when you're called in as a consultant?

I'll say, for example, "Whom are you going to call on this week?"

And the pastor will glance at the chalkboard on the wall or pull out a card and say, "Well, I have seven sick people this week, and then there's a couple of appointments from the new-members class, and I need to see a couple of Sunday school teachers. . . ." He'll pause, then continue, "And I suppose other people will call during the week about various things."

This pastor is basically playing firefighter. He's waiting for the bell to ring (or the axle to squeak, or the Spirit to move). He doesn't see that there is such a thing as taking *initiative* in the area of contacts.

This same person may be conscientious about sermon topics, laying out an annual preaching plan. He may be intentional about selecting themes and texts. But when it comes to people, he's a shepherd waiting for the lost sheep to show up, listening for a call from the wild.

If you take the notion that a church can have a mission (other than shepherding), then you will spend your time in the areas that will bring the greatest payoff. You'll spend it with the key contacts who have the potential to lead others. You'll seek out those who show the greatest readiness to make a decisive commitment at the next interview.

And I've learned you can train pastors to do this — if they're hungry. If someone is content with the reactive style, of course, not much can be done. Shepherding does give a certain sense of worth; you're the rescuer, the one called in when things are desperate. But if a church leader has a vision that goes beyond being well thought of, a vision that includes *harvest*, then some important decisions must be made intentionally.

What are they?

The pastor must say, "Given my limited resources, the most precious of them being my time" (many pastors don't value time as the most precious resource, but it is), "with whom or on what should I be spending it?"

There are two dangers for pastors: Spending too much time getting ready for Sunday, and spending too little time. The right balance gives an optimum quality of sermon and optimum exposure to people who need to be recruited.

I really think the pastor (at least in the average-sized church in America) is still the key person to make people feel they are entering a church legitimately. Frequently it requires no more than a five- to fifteen-minute touch to create a favorable disposition toward the church. From there on, lay people can finish hauling the prospect into the boat. All the pastor needs to do is set the hook.

When I was a pastor, I noticed a curious thing: a fifteen-minute visit with someone would produce a member, while if I spent forty-five minutes, I'd never see the person again! Apparently they got too much of me (or I got too much of them). They must have assumed the expected level of commitment in our church was just too high, and they were frightened away.

If you go to a new bank, and the president takes the trouble to shake your hand, ask your name, and say they'd all be glad to be of service to you, you are impressed. You don't expect the president also to take your money; that's the tellers' job. In fact, you may not see the president once in the next two years. But it doesn't matter; you've been favorably disposed to do your banking there.

The average visitor does not expect nearly as much of the

minister as the average member does. Pastors can get confused about that. They may think outsiders are clamoring for as much attention as the insiders. In most cases, it isn't true. In fact, if pastors give them that much exposure, they can actually choke off their coming toward the church.

This has profound implications for time management.

What other decisions slip past many of the pastors you talk to?

Many are not taking the trouble to educate themselves in needed areas of management.

Almost all ministers are well educated theologically. Most seminary graduates have more to teach than anybody wants to learn. If we spend any time at all preparing for a given sermon, we will meet the needs of the listeners. As Dan Baumann, author of a widely used preaching textbook, says, "Anyone who simply sets forth the text and gives its meaning distinctly will be accused of freshness." *(Laughter)*

Meanwhile, the serious deficiencies are in management and leadership skills.

The question is, how does a pastor gain these skills, short of bringing in Carl George for a week.

Well, that gets expensive! A better approach, for starters, is to subscribe to LEADERSHIP, which does a good job of touching both the theological and management topics of local-church ministry.

Beyond that, you simply have to glean the business fields for concepts that will transfer. An example is Andrew Grove's book of a few years ago, *High-Output Management*. He's the president of Intel, the electronic chip manufacturer. You can get lost in all his jargon, I admit, but the last half of the book is solid-gold stuff on the role of meetings: the one-on-one meeting, the group meeting, the ad hoc meeting, the routine meeting, and so forth.

I know some pastors say, "Well, that's different from how things are in the church," but I believe the God of creation is the one who made organization both necessary and possible. When a fallen world makes organization work, it does so with the principles of truth provided by the Creator.

Do you think more pastors make decisions too quickly or too hesitantly? Are they usually too fast on the trigger or too slow?

That depends on temperament. The biggest problem I see is decision makers not taking the trouble to multiply their options before deciding. Church leaders tend to construe each problem as black or white, either/or, right or wrong, when they need to unravel it a bit. They might see four or five different ways to proceed if they did.

Dave Luecke, a vice-president at Fuller Seminary and a former professor of administrative science, says the English language has a helpful convention along this line in the words *better* and *best*. If I look at a problem and come up with an option, I can say, "I have a good solution." But I cannot say, "I have a better solution," until I have looked at two possibilities. And I cannot claim, "I have the best solution," until I have checked out at least three.

We must get this into our thinking. The best solution is one that has been weighed and selected from an array of potential actions, including whether I should do anything at all. Doctors, in the last thirty or forty years, have been learning that in a lot of cases, they shouldn't do anything. Just give the patient sugar pills and send him home. The body will take care of itself, given time.

How would that work in the church? Let's say, for example, a pastor gets word that a teenager in the youth group was seen drinking. One option is to corner the kid next Sunday and yell at him. What are the other options? Or is this a time to do nothing?

If you feel it's critical for you to represent God's opinion accurately, then you may come out with guns blazing, hitting every target in sight. *God is against teen drinking!*

If, however, you see this as a human behavior with certain causes, you can more accurately decide where to put the medicine. *What is this kid fleeing from? What's he trying to identify with? What hungers, what fears are just beneath the surface? Who are the significant others in his life, and how many of them can I give input to?* Once you study the context, the parents, the peer group, and the teenager himself, you may find the cure belongs nowhere near the symptom. Only after determining the appropriate assignable cause can a good decision be made on how to respond.

The person who reported the incident probably expects you to take out the whip of fury and go after the offender. But if it were that easy, why hasn't somebody already done it?

You might probe to see whether the reporter is even a causal person in the teenager's life. "Who else have you discussed this with? Were they concerned? Are they making any plans? Are you making any plans? You know this teenager; you care enough about him to bring the matter to me. What do you think God may be calling *you* to do?"

You see, if the pastor treats this as a fire call, reaches for his hat, and runs out with sirens blazing, he may be overcome with smoke. How much better to say to the caller, "I'm sort of the coach here, and I'm deeply concerned about this, as you are. Let's get down on our knees right now and pray until we have some insight on what each of us is supposed to do next in this matter."

Pastors have to posture themselves as both caring persons and persons dedicated to the righteousness of God. In a few strict parts of the church today, pastors don't have to show care for people but *do* have to uphold righteousness. In other parts of the church, you have to care about people's feelings whether God is offended or not. I think the best thing to do is to coach people toward redemptive acts rather than just crusade for group moral standards.

And besides, pastors can never forget that people are always testing them. Some of these reports are brought simply to see what will happen. The teenager may *not* have been the one drinking; it may have even been the reporter himself or herself, who wants to know what you'll do. And the way you respond will determine whether you are granted any further franchise for ministry. There are a lot of snares in these kinds of decisions.

Decision making is dangerous, isn't it?
Certainly — especially in this area of "enforcing righteousness." The thing to remember about the prophets who enforced righteousness is that most of them became martyrs!

When a pastor hears about a sheep who has become entangled, the goal is to unsnare him. You may mutter under your breath about the sheep's stupidity, but berating him for being entangled does not produce the deliverance. Beating the thorn bush doesn't help, either. The only effective action is to disengage the sheep.

Once you've multiplied your options, how do you decide the best of the bunch?
That depends on whether you have the gift of wisdom or not. I wish God had given every pastor all the gifts. But then we wouldn't need the body, so we wouldn't have a church.

If a pastor does not have a wisdom gift, he would do well to find someone who does and talk it over. In many of the cases I've counseled, the pastor's wife has the gift he lacks in a critical area. The only question is whether he's willing to consult her.

But God hasn't left his church without what it needs. In other cases, key lay persons have such a gift and are discreet enough to be talked to. The resource is right there in the flock.

There's also a problem of ego, isn't there?
That's right. Leaders don't want to defer, because they hold the power to decide. They forget that even if they defer or delegate, they still have the power to *review*. They can decide:
— that a decision doesn't need to be made
— to make a decision alone

— to make a decision *with* the help of someone else's input and counsel

— that someone else needs to make this decision.

These last two involve the difference between *knowing your mind* and *having your mind made up*. When you know your mind, you know generally where you are on certain elements of an upcoming decision, but you don't know exactly how it ought to come down or what your part should be. When you've made up your mind, you've closed the door to further input.

On certain issues, it's all right to make up your mind — for example, the role your spouse prefers in a congregation. You know your preferences in advance so that when criticism comes, you can respond without flinching.

But in other matters, such as whether to build a new parking lot, you're far better off simply to know your mind as you remain open to this angle and that, weighing the options. You know you intend to minister to more people, and the current space is inadequate, so *something* has to be done. But as you begin, you haven't locked into "We must put fifty more parking spaces where the playing field is now."

In some ways it is best if the pastor arrives at a new action *last* rather than first, after developing broad congregational support. Some decisions need a lot of process attached to them because they are so hard to undo.

That's another part of wisdom, isn't it — knowing which decisions to make unilaterally and which to make corporately?

Yes. I sat with one pastor who was trying to decide how to proceed with planting a daughter church. The problem was, not all of the proponents' attitudes regarding the new mission were wholesome. We spent an hour talking and praying together about how to facilitate the dreams and wishes of these people in an affirming, legitimating way.

We finally came down to "What are the next steps?" At that point, he called in a wise and sensitive staff member, and we tossed it around for another half hour. We explored what actions would keep from hardening attitudes or making people fearful. Because of the lieutenant's input, we wound up with a much different, more seasoned set of steps than if the senior pastor had written them alone or with just me.

This man knew when to stop thinking about the decision himself and call for help. He showed his exceeding wisdom. After I left, the two of them took the plan to a larger group of key lay persons for comment and refinement before proceeding further. The result was a successful launch.

How do you think the wind is blowing these days in terms of who makes church decisions? The North American weathervane swings all the way from strong congregational rule on every detail to strong pastoral initiative.

I think the same trend is happening in the church that is happening in business. Over the last five years, we've seen more and more evidence of a return to direction-giving leadership. The notion that leadership should be shared and democratic has been under revision. The swing is toward a more hierarchical system.

The new authoritative leaders, though, are concerned to be more open to feedback as they go along. They don't want to be cut off or remote. But society does seem to be leaning toward persons of certainty who can call a shot.

Are the assertive leaders getting their feedback more informally than formally?

Not necessarily. Politicians are conducting polls constantly to take the pulse of the people. More and more churches are using surveys to get widespread input.

You know, many of our assumptions are fiction. The effective old-time "dictator" still had his listening posts, his grapevine taps to tell him what was going to succeed and what wasn't. It's the fellow who *didn't* handle those powers sensitively who forms our caricature. But the great empires were built by people who had a good sense of the market, knew where people were and where they were willing to follow. Those rules haven't changed much.

We go through fads of leadership style, with some appearing to be very democratic. David Watson, shortly before his death a few years ago, wrote about sharing the leadership of his church at York, England, and how he came to realize — after some major mistakes had been made — that you simply cannot abdicate leadership in the process of sharing it. The apostolically gifted person still has to be leader among the leaders, or else the ministry goes nowhere.

This is one of the issues where I disagree with some advocates of multiple eldership and so forth. They are afraid of the abuses possible in a hierarchy, and so they want to imagine that there is no gift of leadership, that there are no apostles or evangelists.

But in any given group, the Holy Spirit does not give everyone equal ability to lead. If that is not recognized, there are going to be problems.

We've talked about how pastors don't often get adequate training in decision making. But do pastors enjoy any natural *advantages* when it comes to deciding matters in the church?

Someone has said the chief officer of any group has more ability to discourage something from happening than to make something happen, and that is true of pastors as well. By our *in*attention we can allow almost anything to die if we don't want it to prosper. It takes a strong lay person to come forward and minister month after month, year after year, without encouragement or recognition. The pastor holds the power to bless or wither virtually any part of the church by what he chooses to stroke.

Secondly, pastors have the incredible power of the pulpit to cast vision. Each week they get opportunities to set the tone for the entire congregation. Even more important than the stated topic or Scripture are the illustrations. The pastor's power of illustration and imagery is awesome.

Why is that?
Because illustrations command people's imaginations. There

is no greater force. With negative imagery, pastors can suggest withdrawal; with positive imagery, they can suggest victory. Most don't realize they are artists, painting on the inner canvas of the listeners' minds the scenes that will dominate the life of the whole church.

I sat with a group of ministers who were worried about growth in their denomination. I said, "What do you think? Can you grow?"

"I hope so," said one man, "but I don't know. I preached at one of our conferences recently and said I thought maybe we were dead if we didn't do something pretty soon."

"That sounds like an interesting sermon," I said. "Do you have a copy of it?"

He found a copy, and I took it back to my hotel room. There I spread out the eight pages and began a content analysis. In college I studied a bit of theater, and so I took this sermon apart just like I would a play, noting the various episodes, the climax, the proclimaxes, the anticlimaxes, and so forth. I circled every illustration and examined it for vividness and emotion. The greatest emotional power, as all dramatists know, lies in the themes of life and blood; these move an audience profoundly.

This speaker used one illustration from his childhood about the time his father took him fishing. The first time the boy put his hook in the water, he didn't get a fish but instead a snapping turtle. He excitedly reeled it in.

The father was perturbed, however; he seized his filet knife, grabbed the turtle, and proceeded to saw off its head. He threw the body up on the bank and said, "Now, son, let's get back to fishing."

The preacher went on: "But in a little while, I looked back, and lo and behold, the turtle had righted itself and was walking back down the bank —headless. I said, 'Dad! Dad! The turtle's coming down the bank!'

"And my father said, 'Aw, son, don't worry about him. He's dead; he just doesn't know it yet.' "

This became the speaker's analogy for the denomination!

His audience included a lot of small-town and country people, farmers, weekend fishermen. *Talk about impact!* A Jungian psychologist would go wild just thinking about it. In that one illustration, he planted despair and hopelessness more firmly than any straight-on assertion ever could.

I sat there thinking, *What in the world am I going to say to this group tomorrow morning?* The damage was already done. Once an image is placed in a mind, you can't erase it. All you can do is convert it. What converting power would the gospel have in this case?

I decided to preach on Jesus Christ as the Head of the church. "We are the body of which Christ is the Head," I proclaimed. "And any body that becomes disconnected from the Head *is dead whether it knows it or not*. But in the gospel, life follows the agony of death. The gore of the Crucifixion was not the end; the Resurrection reversed all that. By the suffering and death of Christ, he earned our forgiveness and salvation, and only through the risen Christ do we have the power not to be a dead church.

"What have you done to reunite this body with the Head? What can you do? Are you giving allegiance to the Head? Are you willing to follow his orders? Because apart from him there is no power."

Fascinating.

That pastor didn't know it, but he had used a flame thrower on his audience. He didn't realize what he had done.

The power of the pulpit is a major factor in decision shaping. With it we can school people not to attempt great things for God or to attempt them. We can preset their attitudes in the mold of "we can't" or "we can."

We simply have to think about what we're doing and make intelligent, God-honoring choices.

T E N

MANAGING TIME

We terribly overestimate what we can do in one year and underestimate what we can do in five.

TED ENGSTROM

Never plan to do an hour's work in an hour.

ED DAYTON

Ted Engstrom

Ed Dayton

People want counseling, the sermon needs to be written, the board meeting must be prepared for, the copy machine needs to be repaired, someone needs to be recruited for the fourth-grade Sunday school class — a thousand worthy activities clamor for our time. Each one spends a pastor's time, and once spent, that time cannot be reinvested or recouped. So leaders need to monitor their time investments.

Two of the best "investment counselors" for leaders wondering where to spend their time are Ted Engstrom and Ed Dayton. President emeritus and senior vice-president of World Vision, respectively, the two have led hundreds of "Managing Your Time" seminars, have written several books on the subjects of administration and time management, and are joint authors of Christian Leadership Letter.

Ted Engstrom graduated from Taylor University, was editorial director and general manager of Zondervan Publishing House, and became president of Youth for Christ International before joining World Vision International in 1963.

Ed Dayton graduated from New York University and Fuller Theological Seminary. He worked as an engineer with Sperry Gyroscope and Lear Siegler before joining World Vision in 1967.

What is the most common time-management mistake Christian leaders make?

Ed Dayton: Not planning for tomorrow. The leader is so busy doing things, he or she doesn't take any time to think about the future. Seldom does he realize many of his problems can be solved by taking just 5 percent of his time to ask questions like, "Who can I get to do this job next time? Who can do it better than I can?"

Ted Engstrom: We terribly overestimate what we can do in one year and underestimate what we can do in five. Start by realizing that you can't get out of this mess in one year. But you can lay a foundation that can get you out of this mess in three or five years. By planning now, you can get some control over your time down the road.

Delegation is the word time experts use. In the church, delegation means discipling: training others. Leaders don't do things that others do as well or better.

If delegation is a key to managing time, why do many leaders struggle with it?

Dayton: Given a choice of doing work ourselves or doing work through others, most of us will opt to do it ourselves. Very few people like to manage others. It's hard work with a slow payoff. For example, most of my work is managerial. So I find I enjoy writing the *Christian Leadership Letter* with Ted. We feel we've done something tangible. The rest of the time we're in the management business, and years may go by without knowing if we ever did anything right.

Most pastors are in one-pastor churches. All they have is themselves, some books, an old, beat-up desk, maybe a part-time secretary, and a telephone that rings off the hook. What would you bring to this situation from all you've learned about time management?

Engstrom: Let me make a philosophical introduction to our answer. When you talk about management of time, you're really talking about managing yourself. You cannot learn to repair an automobile solely by knowing how to use a wrench, screwdriver, and pair of pliers. You must first understand how things work overall. Once you gain the comprehensive understanding, you realize it's difficult to tighten a screw with a pair of pliers. That's where time tips can help.

For example, we distinguish between *purpose* and *goal*. Purpose is the general aim you're going for. To give glory to God is a purpose. To preach good sermons is a purpose. A goal, on the other hand, is measurable. To complete writing an outline of my sermon by two o'clock tomorrow afternoon is a goal.

Clearing up this fuzziness helps pastors set goals and utilize their time. Ministry purposes often can't be measured quantitatively; ministry goals can and should be.

Dayton: The first thing I'd do is declare what my goals are. Then I'd ask one or two individuals to hold me accountable in doing my best to achieve them. Second, I would find a prayer partner, a Barnabas who could give me counsel, probably a more mature person than I. Third, I would try to determine my particular gifts. If I were a pastor-teacher, I would build on that. If I were a relationship person, I would build on that.

Let's back up a minute. You talked about people who would hold you accountable. In a one-person pastorate, who might that be?

Engstrom: It may be a mature lay leader, a fellow pastor in the community, or another friend outside the church. Too many pastors start in the ministry with all the capabilities to make the church spin, but they never develop a deep relationship with people who can look at them in a different way than they look at themselves. They look back after ten years and realize that if they'd had counsel at certain points, it would have helped their ministry. For more than a dozen years I've had an accountability group. It has been very meaningful to me.

Dayton: The next step is to take stock of the people in your church. They have spiritual gifts to be tapped. Sometimes people know they have them, sometimes not. Sometimes others see gifts people don't realize they have. Begin to ask people, "What do you think our church is really good at? What can we do well? Who are the gifted people in our church?" Forget the negatives and find the positives. When you begin to hear the same information from three or four people, you know you're discovering the strengths of the church.

This doesn't sound like time management.

Engstrom: But these are the absolutely essential preliminaries. Remember, you have to find out how the pieces work together before you can fix the car. In the church you have to understand the people, their relationship to one another, and how you fit in before it will function effectively and efficiently. Far too many Christian workers unconsciously let work come ahead of their relationships. They put task ahead of understanding.

Dayton: I know a pastor who took a small church of ten families in Washington and decided from the start that nothing was going to happen in that church unless, first of all, someone suggested it and, second, someone volunteered to do it. I happened to be preaching there one day when I saw an example of how this works. Someone came up and made a suggestion to him. He said, "Yes, that's fine." And sure enough, a little later someone came and said he thought he knew how to implement this suggestion and would be willing to try. That church grew because the pastor let the people decide what they could do best and let them go at it.

Engstrom: Once you discover the capabilities of the church and determine a workable leadership style, you can concentrate on practical methods. One thing I'd do as a young pastor would be to keep an appointment book based on twenty-one increments of the week: mornings, afternoons, and evenings, seven days week. Thinking in terms of those twenty-one units rather than every thirty minutes helps avoid being frustrated with the inevitable interruptions. You have an open enough account so you can handle the interruptions, yet still feel comfortable with keeping your calendar.

Dayton: The idea of having twenty-one units also helps you see how much work you're doing. Some pastors may be working twenty out of the twenty-one; that's obviously too much. Eighteen out of twenty-one is too much. This type of calendar helps develop the idea of a standard day. In a typical week, certain patterns will emerge: You're going to be alone to meditate in your study at such-and-such a time; you're going to try to stay uninterrupted for a certain block of time for sermon preparation; you're going to leave some nonscheduled time.

I also suggest letting the board know what you're doing. I know one pastor who went before his board and said, "I want to tell you about a day in the life of your pastor. Here's what I'm doing; this is what I've done for the past two weeks."

So the pastor is in an accountability group, has developed a plan for ministry, and is using a calendar particularly suited to the hectic demands of each week. What are some other things a pastor can do to make ministry more efficient?

Dayton: One of the things we think can be of tremendous help to a pastor is to plan a large number of sermons in advance. It doesn't matter whether you preach them in sequence or not. But why not outline fifty sermons? Set up fifty file folders with subjects and rough outlines; then you've got a place to put ideas when they come to you. In another drawer start a series of folders on your other tasks in the church: a folder for the trustee board, elder board, and the others. This will help you think about your life and the way you're living it in terms of the future, so you plan better.

What about the incredible volume of paperwork?

Dayton: It's not necessary to read everything that comes across your desk. In five seconds I can tell you whether something is worth looking at or not. That's a skill anyone can learn.

Engstrom: Or you can find a retired person to read for you.

He or she can cut out or underline things you ought to read. It doesn't take as long as you might think to teach someone what you're looking for. In two or three hours a week, a volunteer can make a huge dent in your paperwork.

Aren't most of us afraid to let someone else do our reading for fear we'll miss something?

Dayton: Yes, there's the fear something is going to slip through the cracks. I found a psychological way to handle that. I asked myself, "What happens when I'm off camping in the woods for three weeks?" The world somehow gets along without me even though I don't read my mail.

So you miss one out of ten important articles. So what? You have to have a little faith in others. An I-do-it-all attitude really says, "I don't believe in community. I don't believe in other members' gifts." You have to let others help you.

Let's go back to goals. It's fine for the Christian leader to outline one-year, three-year, and five-year goals. But coming into a new situation, he or she is usually faced with well-defined expectations. How does the leader reconcile personal goals with existing expectations?

Engstrom: The first rule is "Don't hurry!"

Dayton: And the second would be "Preach your dreams." I'm not talking about preaching in demanding terms. But if study and prayer have led you to certain convictions about what the expectations of your church or organization should be, then let the Holy Spirit voice those convictions through your preaching. It will take time for the message to get through, but after a year or so, you should begin to see small shifts in attitude.

Sometimes people expect a new pastor to march in and make wholesale changes. They steel themselves to resist. Fool them. Don't change a thing. Wait. Pretty soon they'll come and ask, "When are we going to do so-and-so?" Remember, change takes place only when there is discontent. Your task is to preach holy discontent.

Engstrom: The skills required to get things done through other people can be learned. You can learn to plan, organize, lead, and control. You can learn how to delegate and develop people. Obviously, some people can learn these skills much better than others. But they are learned skills nevertheless. The key is learning to rely on others. For example, you might say to a member of your congregation, "I'm not a very good planner, but I understand that you work for such-and-such a company and that you are involved in planning there. Will you tell me how you do it?" That kind of reliance is a key management principle and also one that fits nicely with the view of the church as a body with many different spiritual gifts.

Once you've found you can learn these skills, practice them. You don't become a good preacher in three or four or five years. You don't become a good manager-leader in three or four or five years either. Sit down in your office and ask, "How old am I? How much experience have I had? What is it that I'm going to have to learn and become skilled at before I can expect to lead these people where God wants them to go?"

Doesn't part of this process include learning how to say no? Traditionally, pastors are supposed to have an open-door policy, being available for every emergency.

Dayton: To a certain extent, being available for emergencies goes with the territory. But you can forestall many interruptions by simply telling your congregation what your standard day is and when you'd like to be left alone for study. If people perceive you to be highly open to interruptions, they'll interrupt you.

A secretary helps a great deal, of course. If you don't have a secretary, or only a part-time one, you might consider a telephone answering machine. Leave this message: "This is Pastor So-and-so. Thanks so much for calling. Right now I have another commitment. I'll be through at eleven o'clock. I'll be happy to call you between eleven and eleven-thirty. If there is an emergency for which you think I should be interrupted, call this number." Then leave the number of someone who lives close to the church and has agreed to take such calls. It can be a different person each day. They can bring the emergency message to the church.

Engstrom: You don't have to be available to everybody all the time. That's poor management. Better management lets people know when you are available.

Pastors who don't manage their time very well often burn out. What are the symptoms?

Dayton: Feelings of unproductivity, discouragement, unsatisfying relationships at home, weariness, and depression. We're seeing more and more of it.

Engstrom: We think one of the major causes is the nature of the church.

A profit-making organization is the easiest to run. It's a business with a narrow measuring stick for success — profit. The next easiest to run is a nonprofit organization like ours, World Vision. We pay our people. We can hire. We can release. There are more problems than with a profit company, but we still have a strong measure of control. Running a volunteer organization like the church is the hardest. The church accepts everyone, warts and all. Yet you're challenging these people to difficult ministry — without pay.

The young pastor coming into the work doesn't realize how difficult this is. And if a businessman says at a church business meeting, "Boy, we ought to run this church like a business," he creates tremendous ambivalence and guilt in this young pastor. You can use some businesslike principles in the church, but you can't run it like a business. It's different.

Dayton: The church is the most complex of all human organizations. It's what we call "goal-conflicted." One goal is to send people forth, and another is to care for them. People are always either getting on a stretcher or getting off — recently hit by disaster or recovering from one, ready to serve. You've got this continual dynamic where relationships, not bottom-line numbers, are the key product. And the number of possible relationships in a church is huge. In a group of 10 people, you have 45 possible relationships. In a church of 100, you have 4,950 possible relationships. That's why pastors must develop processes so the body will care for itself. The pastor alone can't keep up with all the shifting relationships.

Does the body itself need to think in terms of time management?

Engstrom: It could be important. Big corporations like General Motors and AT&T think seriously about corporate man-hours. At World Vision we have six hundred people, and we sometimes think in terms of total corporate time. But as a church, we take time cavalierly. We have all the time in the world, so we tend to relax.

I don't want us to get uptight about the total man-hours we spend (and sometimes waste) in committee meetings and such, but we don't think enough about the value of combined hours from a group of people.

Dayton: Right. We don't train people to lead meetings or to participate in meetings. Too often our meetings don't have agendas, purposes, or goals. I've found every discussion item has three parts: reporting, discussion, action. It helps to announce ahead of time which of these three things will be done at the meeting for each agenda item. Sometimes it will be all three, sometimes only one or two. But announcing it ahead of time aligns everyone's expectations.

I know one lay person who leads meetings very effectively. But the first meeting I attended with her in charge bothered me greatly. If we got stuck on an agenda item, she'd stop the meeting and say, "I think we should pray about this." After prayer she'd sometimes just go on to the next agenda item. The first time it happened I thought, *Boy, what a railroad job that was.* Next month the item was back on the agenda. She was exercising spiritual discipline; when we weren't going to come to an agreement, she moved us on.

Engstrom: The average businessman comes to church meetings and says, "Why can't we make decisions? All day I made decisions at work. Yet I get in this board meeting and spend two hours on what should be a cut-and-dried problem." The businessman forgets that he knows the people at work well. He's with them every day. He sees church board members once a month, and he's already missed three meetings. These people are supposed to agree on things, yet they're coming from twelve different places. It takes time to get to know one another.

Dayton: It also takes time to teach one another what's expected. We often jokingly say that if you want to get something across in a sermon, you need to preach the same sermon six times.

Engstrom: We have an exercise we use at the seminar to help participants get a handle on how they are, and should be, using their time. We ask them to make a list of all the things they're doing and evaluate each one. "How do I feel about that? Am I spending the right amount of time doing it?" Then we ask them to share their lists with a colleague. "How do you feel about what I am doing?" They usually hear some different perceptions of their schedule.

Another exercise is to write the ten most important things you do. Then ask your board, your wife, and your friends to make a list of the ten most important things they think you do. The comparison will probably surprise you.

Dayton: A pastor recently told me his biggest problem is meeting his own expectations. He has an idea of the person he should be when he's forty-five years of age, the size church he should have, and the amount of national influence his ministry should carry. And he's burning himself out trying to meet those expectations, unaware of what others' perceptions of him may be.

Over the years, how have your time management habits changed?

Engstrom: You never fully arrive in the matter of time management. It's a constant struggle. I frequently renew and review my priorities.

If I didn't have my pocket Day-Timer, I would be in trouble. I try to outline my day, my week, and my month, and live with that. But I fail so often in it.

When did you find yourselves becoming aware of the importance of time?

Engstrom: For me it came when I was forty-five. I was president of Youth for Christ, and I realized I was spending too much time on minor matters that were stealing time from important projects. About that time I met Alex MacKenzie. We discovered we were both struggling with problems of time. Out of those discussions, I developed a new perspective on the use of my personal time — and those meetings also led to a book we coauthored, *Managing Your Time*.

Dayton: I've made some monumental mistakes with my schedule. Like Ted, I still struggle with it. I remember a time Ted and I were scheduled to do a "Managing Your Time" seminar in Florida. But my son needed an operation, my missionary daughter was home on furlough, and our other daughter had flown out from the East Coast to be with us. Everything dictated that I stay home, so I said to Ted, "I can't go. You know my priorities. I've got to be here with my son and family." I made a good decision originally.

But the operation went well, and I got to thinking about poor Ted in Florida all by himself. On an impulse I raced to the airport, got on a plane, and after flying all night arrived in Florida the next morning. Exhausted, I did the seminar, but I realized how foolish I had been. My family has never let me forget it.

I take on too much because there are so many fun things to do: teaching, consultations, video projects — creative things I love to do, but don't really need to do. A calendar gets full very fast.

Engstrom: It's easy to say yes to things six to nine months from now. To counteract that tendency, I keep a full-year calendar in my office so I can see and then regulate how full it becomes. Also, every four or five months I take two days with no agenda whatsoever, check into a hotel, and just get my senses together. I may write, read, or just sit and think. It's a time away from people and telephones when I can sort things out and get on track again.

Dayton: I think all of us in the ministry, whatever form, drive ourselves pretty hard. My dad used to say I was a Ford with a Cadillac imagination. We all need to match our workload with our energy level and physical capabilities.

What is the best motivation to help people do something about controlling their schedules?

Dayton: First, discontent. You must get to the place where you're sick and tired of living a hectic life.

Second, prayer. Do what we call fantasizing in prayer. Get away for a day alone somewhere. Bring yourself into God's presence and think about what kind of life you'd like to have fifteen years from now. (If you're eighty now, better make it ten.) Picture in your mind a day in your life. What would you like to do on a typical day fifteen years from now? Imagine yourself getting up in the morning, greeting your family, going to work, and coming home in the evening. Be as detailed as possible. Why fifteen years from now? Because most everything is possible in that time. Then work back into the present. What would you like to be doing ten years from now? Five years from now? At each stage you get more specific as you have to make plans for that fifteen-year ideal. The process will help clarify what it is you really want to be.

Engstrom: Goals motivate us better than anything else. But we realize self-motivation is difficult. I can get our staff moving on certain projects far more easily than I can get myself going.

What are some of the telltale signs that you need to focus on self-motivation?

Engstrom: The easiest one to measure is productivity. Write down in a notebook or journal what you want to accomplish each day. Everything worthwhile needs to be written down. Goals, desires, ambitions, dreams, whatever — write it down so you can review it. I don't accomplish all the things I write down, but if I write it down, I've taken the first step toward doing it. I love to be able to cross out things I've completed.

Dayton: But we always caution people that faster doesn't necessarily mean better. Some time-saving techniques have the capacity to destroy relationships. Every one of us can find ways of doing things in less time. But the question is, "Would our lives still be God honoring and biblical?" You can make a fetish out of saving time.

Occasionally you need to waste some time. Some people come to our seminars who are already way ahead of us. Some are so rigid they need to go to a time-wasting seminar, not a time-saving one. In fact, for the church leaders who come to our seminars, we've devised some very inefficient-sounding advice: Never plan to do an hour's work in an hour. The very nature of ministry means there will always be interruptions.

Give us an example of a particularly well-organized person you've known.

Engstrom: I can think of a disorganized person who accomplished a great deal: Bob Pierce, the founder of World Vision. Bob Pierce was probably as poorly organized as anyone you would ever meet. He hardly knew from one hour to the next what he would be doing. He always had his bags packed ready to go off to Asia or Latin America. But Bob was so Spirit led and personally driven that he was usually in the spots where the need was greatest. He would no more understand what we mean by time management than I understand the mechanics of an airplane. Yet God really used him. Time management is not the only answer to living a productive, redemptive life.

Dayton: I've known many industrial executives who would smile at the elementary nature of the things Ted and I teach about time management in our seminar. For pure personal organization, most industry executives beat us hands down. It's combining some of these time-saving practices with the unique, people-related demands of the ministry that's the trick.

Engstrom: A man who has combined both in his life so well

is Paul Rees. He is disciplined: he's an early riser, has an impeccable filing system, and has catalogued all of the books in his large library. Paul is always prepared. He is a disciplined writer. But although he's an organized person, he's never too hurried to talk to people. You have the feeling you've got his full attention when you're talking to him.

Dayton: In *Chariots of Fire*, all the trainer did was prepare another man to run a race. He wasn't out in front of the crowd. In a sense, he ran his race through the other guy. That's not a bad role for a pastor. I don't think it is *the* role, but it's a good model: building up the rest of the body so it fits together and does what God wants it to do.

ELEVEN

OVERSEEING THE ORGANIZATION

The feeling that you can do the job better yourself makes delegation difficult. But I've been a more effective leader when others have actually done the work.

DONALD SEIBERT

Donald Seibert

Donald Seibert has seen the inside workings of not only churches but high-pressure corporations. As chairman and chief executive officer at J. C. Penney, he gained a reputation as an effective organizer and peacemaker. And in peace, the company prospered.

In 1981, a year when most retailers were taking their lumps, Penney's earnings rose 44 percent on a mere 4.5 percent increase in sales. What was the secret? Business Week pointed to a new management style "keyed to group decision making . . . consensus management."

Seibert, architect of that new atmosphere, is now retired, but his philosophy remains unchanged: develop a team that can continue without a hitch when key individuals leave.

Seibert was vice-president for the White House Council on Families during the Carter years and has served on the Advisory Council for Productivity Improvement.

He's also an active member of Long Hill Chapel in Chatham, New Jersey, where he leads Sunday night congregational singing, teaches Sunday school, lends his voice to various music ministries, and has been an elder and a trustee. For several years, he has also helped lead a small Bible study group of top corporate executives.

Here are his reflections from a lifetime of service within the complex organizations of church and business.

What leadership tensions are common to both business and the local church?

In business, tensions arise when the chief executive's objectives somehow differ from those of long-standing workers in the business. In the church, the same tensions arise when the pastor wants to do one thing, and some of the church pillars — Sunday school superintendent, chairman of the board of elders — want to do something else. The tensions are further compounded by misunderstandings about where the business — or the church — is really heading.

Can you give an example?

I was involved in a church that had a strong commitment to foreign missions — a high-profile missions conference, large missions budget, and so on. A few years after I joined, the pastor was succeeded by another man who shared the commitment to missions but also felt our church's involvement in local ministries was not what it should be. So he tried to motivate us in the direction of local ministries, and his effort was completely misunderstood as a denunciation of foreign missions. The situation grew dramatic, with people raising their voices in meetings. The whole problem could have been avoided if the pastor's intentions had been communicated successfully to all levels of the church.

So pastors have an obligation to articulate direction clearly, to educate the church on what they're trying to do and how they want to do it.

Exactly. At J. C. Penney, whenever our management team prepared to issue a statement, whether it was a press release or an internal memo, we asked ourselves two questions: (1) Is this easily understood? (2) Can this be misunderstood? These questions are quite different, and often our original statement failed the second test and needed to be rewritten.

How do you measure whether you as a leader are getting

your ideas across?

We use a number of techniques: attitude surveys, informal visits by members of the senior management committee, discussions with people at different levels of the company. If you take time to ask questions, you find out quickly what your people understand and do not understand.

Isn't this all rather basic?

Yes. Communication skills are based on common sense. But often they're so simple you ignore them.

Suppose a pastor communicates to a church that God's purpose for them is to live holy lives and preach the gospel to the world. They decide to send out _x_ number of missionaries, build new Sunday school facilities, etc. What happens next?

First, as the pastor, I would want to know exactly how equipped I am to handle these ministry goals. If Sunday school facilities are inadequate and need expanding, I put that down as a goal. If my missionary outreach needs expansion, I put that down. I find out how financially able the church is to meet these goals, and whether we have the potential to raise the money. I ask specific things like, "Is labor available in the church?" "Will we have to hire outside help?"

Then I ask some more difficult questions: "How many people are committed to these broad ministry objectives? Where is the support going to come from?" If I don't have a lot of people behind me, it would be foolish to go ahead with a building program. Instead, the first objective would be to spend a year doing nothing but building support and developing understanding for the programs within the church. It's absolutely critical to know you and your people are together in your goals and objectives.

Good sports teams have at least two things in common: a coach or quarterback who calls good plays, and players who understand their assignments. It's interesting that a team that works together without a highly visible star will usually beat the team that depends solely on the superstar.

Finally, I'd try to keep goals simple and within reason. To illustrate, I've worked with several volunteer choirs. A group of amateur singers may not be able to do justice to some of Handel's music, but if you select material within their level of competence, they sound magnificent. It may take lots of time and effort, but you can gradually raise their level of competence. Perhaps in a few years, you'll be able to come back and have these people sing Handel.

Is there a difference between *management* and *leadership*?

Here's a distinction I make. Management is the process of assuring that the programs and objectives we have set are implemented. Leadership, on the other hand, is the process of motivating people.

Both are strategic skills, for business people like myself and for pastors, too. Every pastor needs to know what he has to work with before any work can get done. This means taking inventory of resources, understanding the congregation's strengths and weaknesses, reviewing all personnel — the human resources — noting where they're placed, and eliminating structural impediments. These are basic management tools.

If a pastor or a business person is not strong in motivating, he can enlist key people who have demonstrated over time that they have influence with others. If you can identify these people and get them committed to your objectives, they can help sell your programs and motivate others to put them into effect.

What management principles tend to be missed by the local church?

In the churches I've attended, one of the biggest conflicts has been between lay stewardship leaders and lay spiritual leaders — typically the trustees versus the elders. Ideally, trustees raise and manage money and tangible resources; elders provide spiritual leadership. These two functions aren't mutually exclusive, but too often lay people can't see how their goals and objectives are common. It's a chronic problem.

Any solutions?

Well, let me tell you what we did at Penney's. We used to agree on our main objectives and then turn each division loose to plan: the retail division produced a plan, the buyers produced a plan, marketing produced a plan, and so on. Even though we were all working from the same objective, we often found things just didn't mesh. We weren't synchronized. And when the results weren't productive, we had a lot of finger pointing as to whose plan failed.

We moved to a team-management approach. We gathered the leaders from each division into a room and said, "Don't come out until you've produced one harmonious plan." Not only did we start to get good results, but the finger pointing stopped, because each leader was co-author of the plan.

I don't want to oversimplify, but is there any reason why the same principle can't work in the church? The boards of elders and trustees, for instance, could put together leaders from both boards and produce one good plan. Of course, for the plan to work, *all* board members must fully understand the plan and be sold on it. Again, communication must prevent misunderstanding.

What about the oft-repeated line "You can't run a church like a business"? In what way should business principles *not* be brought into the church?

Businesses exist to make financial profit; without profit the business dies, and no other objectives can be accomplished. So I would say that in running a church, you should not use business *objectives.*

But in administering church programs, you should consider using good business *principles.*

One of those principles is to treat people with respect. I believe it's not only questionable morally but counterproductive to run over people in any kind of situation, church or business. You may produce short gains that way, but you'll pay the price down the road in alienated and departed parishioners.

Is the pastor the chief executive officer of the church in the same way as a CEO is in a corporation?
I think the pastor is the church's CEO, but the two positions are not parallel. As the CEO of a corporation, everyone reports to me either directly or indirectly. The CEO of a church is more like the CEO of our nation — the President. He leads, but only with our consent.

What do you expect from the pastor in this unique leadership role?
I expect the pastor to be the initiator of clearly defined, easily understood spiritual goals. I don't expect him to develop all the programs to accomplish these goals, but he has to initiate them.

Over the years, have your various pastors successfully done this?
Not all of them. In some places I was never sure, not only of what I was expected to do in the church but of where the church was going in general.
In fact, if you asked the members of a typical congregation to write in twenty-five words or less where they think their church is headed, you'd get many different answers.

In addition to the role as initiator, how does the pastor function as church administrator?
The buck stops with the pastor, who must assume final responsibility for the way the church is administered. That's not to say every pastor is a good administrator. You have other functions to perform, and you'd probably like to spend more time on sermon preparation and counseling, for instance. But, regardless, you have to be accountable for how the church is run. You can delegate administration, but you can't delegate accountability. The big danger in delegating

administration — if you then walk away from it — is that the wrong administrator can gradually change the whole program of your church.

Does that mean a pastor must supervise each ministry of the church?

Certainly not. I feel I've been a more effective leader when others have actually done the work. And I want everyone to know who accomplished what. It's the same with pastors. The feeling that you can do the job better yourself makes delegation difficult. But delegation is a must in any organization, and I believe people will execute a plan more successfully if it's *their* plan too.

As a leader, how do you overcome the feeling that you can do the job better yourself?

That's not easy to answer. I think it's a given that the pastor will not be the most skilled person in the church at everything. Otherwise he'd be leading the choir, singing the solos, and running the air conditioning. In my company, I can find someone who is better than I am at performing almost every function. Marketing, advertising, writing product specifications — you name it, someone can do it better.

But a symphony conductor is not usually the best French horn player, and he doesn't feel threatened. His role is to make the whole orchestra function to its potential. You should not feel threatened by an individual with great administrative skills, for example. Use him; help him realize his potential within the church.

But what happens when the French horn player only wants to play solos? Doesn't participatory leadership encourage that kind of thing?

I suppose in some cases it does. But then you have the other side: When a number of people participate in leadership and administration, *they* help deal with the would-be soloist. The responsibility doesn't rest entirely on *your* shoulders. Furthermore, in my church experience, most problems of this nature sprang from spiritual problems within the individual. They weren't the result of management styles at all.

So you're democratic as opposed to autocratic?

I am careful not to be autocratic. True, many organizations prosper under an autocratic leader. But in those places, you'll also find a lot of unhappy people. When they find they just can't work in that kind of environment, they leave.

And in a church with an autocratic pastor, a large part of the congregation becomes so dependent on this type of leader that when he steps down, he's almost impossible to replace. One of the principal responsibilities of a CEO is to assure the company that an appropriate successor is ready to step in if something happens. There can be no interruption of the company's growth. This is hard to pull off in companies led by an autocratic leader. In a sense, it is much better if my organization doesn't depend on me as an individual but rather on my part in the long-range goal-setting process. And when I leave, this process must go on.

If I don't have strong management skills, can I still lead effectively?

Yes, if you recognize that management does need to happen in your church. And just because you've never worked with management principles and tools doesn't mean you can't learn. Pastors are formally educated people; they have the basic intellect to understand these things. I believe many pastors would surprise themselves by discovering what good administrators and managers they really are. We all know people who became good golfers past the age of fifty. They never knew they had the talent.

My own formal education was not in business administration. I know highly successful business people who have degrees in music, English, and philosophy. Administrative skills were picked up along the way.

Can you summarize your leadership principles for pastors and other church leaders?

I believe organizations improve when you do the following:

— Understand your own objectives, your own sense of mission and goals.

— Clearly articulate those objectives to your lay leaders, and try to get some feedback as to how well they understand them.

— Exercise patience. It will take time before you have enough of your parishioners behind you to turn objectives into working programs.

— Take inventory of your personal resources and those available within your congregation.

TWELVE
BUILDING SPIRITUAL UNITY

It is impossible to muscle unity in a church.

TRUMAN DOLLAR

Truman Dollar

Fundamentalist churches suffer from many stereotypes, but unity isn't one of them. The common image is usually one of scraps and splits. But if Truman Dollar isn't careful, he's likely to change that image.

During his sixteen-year pastorate at the Kansas City (Missouri) Baptist Temple, he saw the all-white congregation become racially integrated and at the same time grow to an average attendance of 1,800.

In 1984 he went to the ten-thousand-member Temple Baptist Church in the Detroit suburb of Redford. In addition to directing the diverse ministry there, he writes a monthly column for the Fundamentalist Journal, often calling into question divisive practices among Christians.

The son of a Baptist minister, Dollar began preaching at age fifteen. He graduated from the University of Missouri, where he was president of both the honor society and the student body, then served churches in Florida, Missouri, and Michigan before becoming senior pastor in Kansas City in 1968.

In this discussion, the first of three addressing tasks unique to the pastoral leader, Dollar offers counsel on how to bring solidarity and concord to a church.

With all the other concerns facing pastors, is establishing unity all that important?

Unity is vitally important if for no other reason than the fact it validates the gospel. There aren't many things more important than that.

You can't expect to win people to Christ when the body is fragmented and warring.

When Jesus prayed in John 17 that the church be unified, what kind of unity was he referring to? Doctrinal unity? An emotional affection for one another? A sense of common mission?

In the New Testament, the church had to decide whether it would include both Jews and Gentiles. It had to decide if men and women would both be involved. It had to decide if it was a church for free men and slaves. From Acts 15 and Galatians 3:28, we understand the church clearly decided it would include them all. It opted for diversity. Yet in that diversity, it clearly had unity. I see three types.

1. *Functional unity* involves the church's organizational tools: gifted leaders, structure, its goals, and its mission — carrying the gospel around the world, baptizing people, and discipling them.

2. *Doctrinal unity.* There were some limits beyond which you could not go, such as accepting the teaching of the Judaizers or the Libertines. The early church leaders talked a lot about heretics. They were willing to disrupt temporarily the church's unity to create a stronger, lasting unity of doctrine. They insisted that grace must be taught.

3. The church's *spiritual unity* is captured in Jesus' summary of the Law: loving God with all your heart, soul, mind, and strength, and loving your neighbor as yourself.

Spiritual unity has a vertical dimension, a unity with God — holiness. The Bible lists sins that God hates, which break our unity with him — uncleanness, filthiness, whoremongering — behaviors and lifestyles that affect the purity of the church.

Spiritual unity also has a horizontal dimension, a humble

regard for others that overcomes schisms. For example, in Philippians Paul calls divisions carnal; he reprimands Euodia and Syntyche; and he begs them to have the humility, the servant mind, of Christ. Spiritual unity is by far the most difficult of the three.

Is this kind of unity possible, or in a fallen world do we have to settle for something less?

I don't think we ought to look for less. That would be like saying, "We're going to keep only nine of the Ten Commandments," or "We're going to give 8 percent instead of a full tithe." Neither do I think we should say, "Some disunity is acceptable."

Complete unity is what we're after. Yet in a fallen world you constantly have people like Diotrephes in the church, and you have to deal with them because they disrupt a church's unity.

We have never achieved perfect unity in a local church any more than any of us has been completely transformed into the image of Christ. It is a process that is ongoing, one that will not be realized ultimately until Jesus comes back. But that is the goal. To be willing to accept less is sin.

What does unity in the church look like? Can you think of a specific time when you saw it, at least in embryonic form?

I was on the staff of the Kansas City church for twenty-three years, seven as an associate and sixteen as senior pastor. At one point I'd spent half my life there. One Sunday morning I stood up and said, "A family in our church is about to lose their house unless they receive two thousand dollars by the end of the day. You don't need to know who they are, but trust me that they're godly people. We're not going to vote on it. If you feel strongly about this, I'll be at the door following the service, and you can stop and give me a check."

Before the service my wife had said, "Are you going to set a bad precedent?"

I said, "I don't know. All I know is that I'm hurting because this family is going to lose its house."

Before the day was over, people had given over two thousand dollars. When I announced it, there was a sense of euphoria in the congregation. Together we had done something bold and creative to help someone and hadn't worried about setting precedents.

Another incident involved three men, one Caucasian, one Hispanic, and one black. All three worked at TWA, and all three hated each other. Then, within six months or so, all three of them began attending the church.

About fifteen years later in a testimony meeting, Sam, the black man, stood up. Here's a guy who had been involved with the NAACP. When Martin Luther King, Jr., was shot, he flew to Atlanta for the big march at Emory University. Sam said, "I remember when I used to look at Bill and Augie and despise them because of my racism. And now we meet at lunch for prayer." Bill and Augie both stood and confirmed how meaningful they found those prayer times. All three had come to the same church, all three had become Christians, and all three in one testimony meeting got up and talked about being reconciled in Christ.

Can you strategize harmony? Does it require planning and forethought? Or is it simply a gift from God quite unrelated to human effort?

As we teach people to develop the mind of Christ, we build unity. But it is impossible to muscle unity in a church. Unity doesn't begin with strategies; it begins with people. Personhood precedes program.

Yet the way we do things does make a difference. If I do not have integrity as a leader, if I do not model the mind of Christ, unity won't happen in the congregation, because the things that help produce unity won't flow out of my life.

Let me illustrate. One thing I do is insist on giving the congregation sufficient information about the church's finances. I want them to know how resources are being allocated and that their money is being handled well. This helps prevent disunity. But that wouldn't happen if I didn't care about honesty and integrity.

So unity in a congregation doesn't come from the members up. It comes from the leaders down.

Yes. I believe God has ordained a vehicle to accomplish unity: gifted leaders (Eph. 4:11–12), men and women who know the power of the Holy Spirit. What happens in the church begins with its leaders. As a natural result of these leaders exercising their leadership function, unity flows.

A church can be diagrammed in what I call *concentric circles of commitment.* At this church, the center circle includes the pastoral staff and chairman of the deacons. The next circle out from the center is the finance committee. The next circle, the deacons. Then the Sunday school superintendents, then the Sunday school teachers, then those who come Sunday night and Wednesday night, and so on, all the way to the periphery. When I teach about the unity of the body, or give out financial information, or do anything, I start with the core. They become informed and committed and help me reach out and include the next circle and then the next. It ripples outward until the entire church is discipled and informed.

What's the biggest impediment to unity that you face?

Autonomy. The opposite of unity is not disunity as much as autonomy. By that I mean individuals refusing to submit to the teaching of the Scripture by the gifted leaders whom God gave authority.

How do the gifted leaders avoid becoming autonomous themselves?

Paul tells Timothy, "Take heed unto thyself, and unto the doctrine." You have to be careful to submit yourself to the doctrine given by God. You also have to submit yourself to other leaders the church has ordained.

In what areas is unity most difficult to achieve?

The racial issue is the most difficult by far. When I came to the church in Kansas City, it was not racially integrated. I began to teach these principles, and within two years we accepted our first black family. When I left almost sixteen years later, we had a black deacon who in the last election received more votes than anyone else. Progress comes slowly.

Here at Temple Baptist, we're still struggling with the racial issue. Minorities make up about 18 percent of the student body of our Christian school. In sixty years we had never had a black preacher speak — until 1985. Dr. S. M. Lockridge was one of the highlights of our summer Bible conference. We have a few blacks in the morning service every week, and at least we now receive members without regard to race, but the problem is not overcome. That eats at me, because I understand it's a spiritual dysfunction. It's not something we work on just for the public or the media.

In working for oneness within a congregation, what's been the price tag for you personally?

First of all, there is an incredible investment of emotional energy, an investment of yourself. This is true regardless of the church's size, though it certainly becomes more difficult as the church gets larger. The *Dallas Morning News* once interviewed W. A. Criswell and asked, "How can you possibly know twenty-five thousand people?"

Criswell answered, "I know two groups of people in this church — all the key leaders and all the kooks."

This church has ten thousand members, with about three thousand average attendance. Every Sunday I shake hands with a thousand people. Each week a lady prepares for me a list of ten families, with their pictures and brief biographies. I memorize them, and the next Sunday I pick out those ten families and greet them. All of this builds personal credibility so you can invest yourself in their lives spiritually, and ultimately, it helps bring unity.

I also pay a huge emotional price when someone is disrupting the body, especially when I must confront moral impurity. I believe in confrontation, but I pay the price when I have to meet someone and say, "I understand this is true, and as Matthew 18 commands, I want to talk with you about it."

One of the toughest confrontations is with a person who has a chronic negative attitude. It's difficult to call that a church discipline case. How do you act in situations that are not clear-cut moral violations?

Several years ago an executive for a large corporation served on our finance committee in Kansas City. He was a bright man, but for two years he constantly brought up petty criticisms: "You're 1 or 2 percent over budget in disbursements." I listened, tried to give him information, and reasoned with him. But he kept carping, and that pains you when you know you're not doing anything outrageous or ethically wrong.

I finally called the comptroller of the huge corporation where this man worked. I asked him what budgeting margins they maintain and found they weren't anywhere near their projections. They'd projected a break-even year and in the first six months lost $88 million.

So I confronted this man in the presence of the finance committee, not as a smart aleck, but simply to say, "Don't demand standards of us that your own industry cannot maintain. Be reasonable." That was painful, but it had to be done. The man finally resigned, which was a good thing, though I don't like that ever to happen. He simply began to realize he was a continual irritant and nobody was paying attention to him any longer.

Would you say that most discord starts with this kind of personality wrinkle, rather than significant theological differences?

Disunity rarely comes from legitimate theological disagreements. It comes from people who are acting autonomously, who are not obeying the Scripture: "Let this mind be in you which was also in Christ Jesus." That's where Paul had most of his problems.

What's the difference between being autonomous and being a strong, independent thinker? You want people in the con-

gregation who can take initiative.

Instead of calling them independent, I call these people secure in Christ. People who are secure in Christ offer some of the brightest and most helpful ideas for the growth of the church. And they can be aggressive.

But here's the difference: They offer ideas, do homework, take initiative, and still maintain the mind of Christ. When the body has made its decision, they don't continue to lobby or create dissent. The autonomous person, on the other hand, maintains his position long after the vote and says, "You're all wrong."

Has there been a time when you have had to be "the secure Christian," when you wanted one thing and the church acted counter to that?

Not officially, because of my style of leadership: I don't allow a vote until I see we're unified. I refuse to maintain my autonomy by going into a meeting with a strong design and forcing a vote on policy decisions. We discuss it and work it over until we reach a consensus. In sixteen years as senior pastor in Kansas City, I had only one negative vote as a result.

Of course, this means I may change my position radically during the course of a meeting. We wanted to build a new center some years ago, and I was ready to go. I went into the meeting with an entire finance plan laid out. But during the discussion, I realized, as they did, it was too soon, and we backed off. We ended up waiting two more years. But I didn't go home from those meetings offended.

Naturally we do not extend that flexibility to the cardinal doctrines of Scripture. But on other matters, I try to avoid being adversarial.

Do new pastors usually have to wait several years before the congregation rallies around them and their vision for the church?

You can expect disagreement at the outset of most pastorates. When I became senior pastor in Kansas City, I had not chosen any of the staff members. So they didn't have my mindset. But time is usually on the pastor's side. Over the years, they adopt the pastor's mindset and goals or they feel increasingly uncomfortable. If a staff member cannot adjust after some years, he generally chooses to leave.

Time also helps resolve other problems. Since I've been in Detroit, we've had several hundred families join the church. These people came partly because they respond to my style of preaching and leadership. So the longer a pastor stays, the more likely the church will assume his philosophical image through a natural process. Other members remain because pastor and people mutually adjust.

How might a pastor inadvertently contribute to *disunity* in the body?

One of the biggest problems is the inability to shift roles in ministry. It's a weighty thing to stand in the pulpit on Sunday with this Book in your hand, representing God. And it's tough to shift from that role.

You walk in Monday morning and tell a secretary, "Order a trainload of paper clips."

The secretary says, "Are you sure we need a trainload?"

You think, *You're talking to God's man. Yesterday I stood with the Book in my hand with an infallible message.* Some pastors simply are not able to shift gears and understand that on Monday morning the secretary may have infinitely more information about how many paper clips to order than the pastor does.

When pastors are unable to make the role shifts gracefully, they create dysfunction in authority roles. A pastor goes home to his children and he is still the pastor because he can't shift roles. It ends up that the child has neither a parent nor a pastor. That causes a dysfunction in the home. In a church, it breeds disunity.

Another danger is what David Jeremiah calls the "I-thou" approach to preaching, that somehow what I say from the pulpit as the representative of God applies to you but does not apply to me. So I can preach against sin but somehow be involved in it at the same time. We've all been shattered in recent years by the number of casualties in the ministry from this mentality. When a person stands in the pulpit and says, "Here's what God said," but doesn't let that affect him in any way, congregations are fractured.

Are some issues worth standing for even if they cost the church its unity?

I am willing to die for what Dr. Bob Ketcham used to call the "irreducible minimum" — the gospel message, the redemptive work of Christ, the inspiration of Scripture.

I am willing to split a church for the integrity of the institution — in my case, Baptist distinctives.

On practically everything else, I am not willing to fight. Take eschatology. I'm strongly pre-trib, pre-mill, but many matters of eschatology are just not that clear, so I tolerate other viewpoints while I preach what I believe the Bible teaches.

Do you often preach on the theme of unity?

I preach on it but don't call it that.

Then how do you approach it?

I cover the biblical principles about loving one another. And I talk about the fundamentalists who blast each other in the periodicals. I really raise the Devil about that.

One means of trying to build loyalty is talking up the threat of attack. "We are the remnant people and some group out there is persecuting us." Is that a valid method?

I think a lot of anticommunist preaching, for example, has been in many cases a unity-building and fund-raising tool. I am willing to concede that some of this is unconscious. As Eric Hoffer observed over twenty-five years ago in *The True Believer*, "It's easier to unify people through hate than through love."

I've seen people milk those crusades and then I have seen

their organizations fall apart because either the issues are removed or people lose their intensity. You don't build a church based on your opposition to abortion or pornography or your hatred of Keynesian economics. I'm not going to put my neck on the line for some political candidate and then find that the expletives have to be deleted. *(Laughter)*

The foundation of the church can't be an anti-something crusade. You build it on the redemptive work of Christ.

How has your thinking on unity changed over the years?

I was on my first church staff at age nineteen and started pastoring at twenty-one. I realize now my ministry was basically strategizing how to outsmart people. I didn't understand body life; I didn't understand the gifts. I felt there was a difference between pastors and lay people in *essence*, not just function. So in my early ministry I had a lot of conflict. Unity was something I had to manipulate.

Fortunately or unfortunately, I was on the varsity debate team at the University of Missouri for three years. I was a good debater, and I let a lot of that creep into my leadership. I could outtalk anybody whom I pastored. I won a lot of battles. But I lost a lot of wars. I thought I had to win every time to maintain leadership.

I got tired of that. I realized it was hollow. I began to see what the Bible said and understand the Spirit of God had to bring unity as I faithfully taught people. It took time, but I have changed dramatically. I finally got to where I could say to a group of deacons, "You know, I really blew it." I learned I could make mistakes of judgment as an administrator, and when I admitted them, there was nobody to fight with. They would say, "We understand. We make mistakes, too."

So the urge to be right can block unity.

You don't have to be the repository of all truth to be a leader. You can be vulnerable and admit before a crowd, "I have made some mistakes and I've learned by them." Chuck Swindoll is probably the greatest at this. He knows just how far to go, to be vulnerable without simply dumping on people. I heard him tell a story about himself when he was accused of shoplifting that was a great teaching tool.

I told this church once about some incidents during my early ministry. I had great success in building projects. The church built 421 units of senior citizens' homes. The whole project was worth twelve or thirteen million dollars. I began to realize I was good at financial management, and so with a couple of men in the church I got involved in a number of business ventures. They were moderately successful.

Nobody said a word to me, but I became deeply convicted that as a minister of the gospel, I needed to live by the gospel. I read those passages about being a soldier of Jesus Christ, and I just up and sold all my shares voluntarily. I never told anybody except my wife. Eight or ten years had to go by before I could admit I'd gotten so involved in that.

Preachers don't often admit they've made mistakes. I can understand that. I don't want to stand up and tell all the dumb and sinful things I've done. But if I don't open up, I often can't help people. So I've got to be transparent.

What was a mistake you made that caused a lot of disunity?
When I was a young preacher, twenty-one years old, I took a little church of about thirty-five people in Fort Lauderdale, Florida. I led the church up to about two hundred, but the offerings were poor. We were running up deficits, yet I was dead set on having an additional staff member anyway. I figured everything had to be bigger and better and growing faster than the church down the street—you know, common nonsense. I got my way but ultimately lost the church. They didn't fire me, but I left because I saw the growing deficit. I was unwilling to admit I was wrong and being foolish.

Experiences like that helped me realize I'm not right every time. And I don't have to assert myself or lose my leadership every time. So now, instead of trying to manipulate unity, I try to just teach and model the mind of Christ, function as a leader, and let the Spirit of God bring unity.

In our church we have two little boys named Nick Maple and Frankie Galloway. One is four and the other is five. Both of them, in three months' time, came down with leukemia. I've seen our whole church rally around those boys in a very moving way.

Families have taken food for months. I've seen our families pour into the hospitals. I've seen them weep on a Sunday morning as we kneel, three thousand together, to pray for Nick and Frankie. The unity has been overwhelming to me. And it just arose. There was a functional unity, a doctrinal unity, and a spiritual unity preceding it that made it possible.

T H I R T E E N

GIVING SPIRITUAL GUIDANCE

Pastoring in the twentieth century requires two things: One, to be a pastor, and two, to run a church. They aren't the same thing.

EUGENE H. PETERSON

Eugene H. Peterson

T he pastor is not precisely like any other leader — not CEO, not physician, not attorney, not social worker. The pastor rightly marches to a different drumbeat.

And that's the challenge for **pastors** who lead. They cannot march lockstep with the methods of corporations and secular nonprofit organizations. No one outside the pastorate fully understands its own unique cadence.

In his twenty-four years as pastor of Christ Our King Presbyterian Church in Bel Air, Maryland, Eugene Peterson has done a lot of thinking about pastoral work: What is it? What keeps us from it? How is it done?

The answers? Eugene doesn't know if there are hard and fast answers, but he agreed to talk about the problems.

Eugene developed his approach to pastoring from scriptural study and personal experience, and he explains it in his well-crafted **Five Smooth Stones for Pastoral Work** (John Knox), and his many articles for LEADERSHIP.

He's a man who reads mysteries, runs marathons, goes for long hikes in the woods with his wife — and who doggedly applies himself to the essentials of pastoral work.

How did you develop your view of the pastoral role?

One of the worst years I ever had was in the early days of this church. Our building was finished, and I realized I wasn't being a pastor. I was so locked into running the church program I didn't have time to be a pastor. So I went to the Session one night to resign. "I'm not doing what I came here to do," I said. "I'm unhappy, and I'm never at home."

The precipitating event was when one of my kids said, "You haven't spent an evening at home for thirty-two days." She had kept track! I was obsessive and compulsive about my administrative duties, and I didn't see any way to get out of the pressures that were making me that way. So I just said, "I quit."

How did they react?

They wanted to know what was wrong. "Well," I said, "I'm out all the time. I'm doing all this administrative work, serving on all these committees, and running all these errands. I want to preach, I want to lead the worship. I want to spend time with people in their homes. That's what I came here to do. I want to be your spiritual leader; I don't want to run your church."

They thought for a moment and then said, "Let *us* run the church." After we talked it through the rest of the evening I finally said okay.

Two weeks later the stewardship committee met, and I walked into the meeting uninvited. The chairman of the group looked at me and asked, "What's the matter? Don't you trust us?"

I admitted, "I guess I don't, but I'll try." I turned around and walked out. It took a year to learn to trust God to call and use the men and women around me in ministry.

I do moderate the Session. And I tell other committees that if they want me to come for a twenty-minute consultation on a specific problem I'll be happy to do that. But I haven't been to a committee meeting now, except in that capacity, for seventeen years.

Doesn't every pastor have to be an administrator, even if that's not his gift?

Every pastor has to make sure administration gets done. If you can't see to it that it does get done, you're in trouble. Pastoring in the twentieth century requires two things: One, to be a pastor, and two, to run a church. They aren't the same thing. Every seminary ought to take their pastoral students and say, "Look, God has called you to be a pastor, and we want to teach you how to be pastors. But the fact is that when you go out to get a job, chances are they're not going to hire just a pastor, they're going to hire somebody to run the church. Now, we'll show you how to run a church, and if you master what we're telling you, you can probably do it in ten to twelve hours a week. That's the price you're going to pay to be in the position of pastor."

What are some of the things you do to pay the price?

I return telephone calls promptly. I answer my mail quickly. I put out a weekly newsletter. I think that's essential. When the parish newsletter comes out once a week, the people sense you're on top of things; they see their names and what's going on. It's good public relations. If you want to keep your job, people have to believe the church is running okay.

Apparently for the last seventeen years it has been, though you haven't been "running" it.

I suppose it's the trust between the elders and me. They don't always do it the way I want them to, but when I decided I wasn't going to run the church, I also had to decide that if they were going to run it, they would have to do it their way, not mine. They listen to my preaching, are part of the same spiritual community, and know the values being created and developed, so I trust them to run the church in the best way they know how. Sometimes I do get impatient, because it's not the most efficient way to run a church. A lot of things don't get done.

Because they are volunteers?

Partly. Some of the leaders aren't fully motivated. A congregation elects elders and deacons, and sometimes chooses them for the wrong reasons. Some are only marginally interested in the life of the church, so they have neither the insight nor the motivation to be productive. I can either give them the freedom to fail, or else step in and train people to be exactly what I want them to be. I've chosen to leave them alone.

You also have volunteer secretaries. How has that worked?

Wonderfully! The idea came to me while I was reading a Dorothy Sayers mystery. Peter Wimsey is out trying to solve a murder, and he's having a difficult time getting information. Nobody will talk to him because he's an outsider. So he searches for someone who would know the community, locates an elderly spinster, and hires her as a typist. Then he has her employ a typing pool, and these ten to fifteen people are his links to the community.

I thought, "That's exactly what I need." So I asked a woman whom I thought was competent in these areas to be the church office coordinator. We found two people for each weekday to work from nine to two o'clock, and informed the congregation of the new office hours. We divided up the office work to specific days and defined the responsibilities for each person. We have to plan ahead a little; we can't get things done immediately. But the plus part is that we developed a lot of ministry. They do a lot of listening, they're in touch with many people, and they tell me things that are going on. They are important to the running of the church.

Do these ideas make a difference in how your people view the church? Do they draw the community together?

Community to me means people who have to learn how to care for each other, and in one sense, an efficient organization mitigates against community, for it doesn't tolerate you if you make mistakes. This is not the situation in the church. We have inefficiency on our church office staff, but efficiency is not nearly as important as being patient with people and drawing them into a mutual sense of ministry. It's the way we operate; everything doesn't have to be "out today." If work is planned well enough, there's room for things to wait.

Walk us through one of the inefficient things you allowed to happen, even though many leaders would see it as an administrative lapse.

I recall the case of a woman who was working in a voluntary capacity coordinating several closely related programs. When she started out, she was excited about it and did a good job. But as time went on, she dipped into other things and began doing her job indifferently. I was dealing with her as her pastor on family problems, and I felt it was important for me not to criticize her administration or ask her to resign. So I didn't do anything.

Matters became worse. I had many phone calls and listened to many complaints. I said, "I'd like to improve the situation, but I can't promise anything." I just waited with it and kept on being a pastor to her. I felt that to keep from compromising my position as pastor to her, I had to let the programs in a sense fail that year and suffer with poor administration. Many pastors wouldn't have permitted that, and for their ministry styles it might have been correct for them to step in and administratively handle the situation. I'm not against that kind of efficiency by any means, but I need to know what I'm good at.

I have to pay the price of being good at certain things and not be a jack-of-all-trades.

How do you make sure that personal ministry happens?

For one thing, I do home visitation. I do it on a sense of need, when I know there's something special going on in someone's life. Birth, death, loss of job, relocation, or trouble in the home are good indicators for me to visit. I talk with them, listen to their problems, find out where they are, and pray with them. That's the advantage of pastoral work; it can

respond to all the little nuances of community life and participate in them.

There's a line in a poem about a dog going along the road
with haphazard intent. Pastoral life is like that. There's a sense
of haphazardness to it, for me anyway, because I don't want
to get locked into systems where I have to say, "No, I'm too
busy to do that; I can't see you because I have this schedule."
But the haphazardness is not careless; there is purpose to it.

**Does the pastoral role come straight from the Word, or has
time changed its criteria?**

A hundred or so years ago, pastors had a clear sense of
continuity with past traditions. You knew you were doing
work that had integrity; your life had recognized value and
wholeness. Today, that's just not true. We're fragmented into
doing different things. On the other hand, in the pulpit you *do*
have that sense of continuity. When I'm preaching, I know
I'm doing work that has continuity back to Isaiah. I prepare
sermons somewhat the way Augustine and Wesley prepared
sermons. I'm working out of the same Scriptures, so I don't
feel third-rate when I'm in the pulpit.

During the week, however, I do feel looked down upon.
When I go to the hospital to visit, for example, I'm a barely
tolerated nuisance. Other factors contribute to this feeling of
uselessness. When you have serious problems running your
church, what do you do? You call up a company and have
them send out somebody to show you how to run a duplicat-
ing machine, or you take a course in church management.
And who teaches you? Somebody from the business community. All through the week it seems we're intimidated by
experts who are teaching us how to do our work — but they
don't know what our work is. They're trying to make us
respectable members of a kind of suborganization they're
running, and as a consequence, we develop a self-image
that's healthy only on Sunday. I think pastoral work should
be done well, but I think it has to be done from the inside, from
its own base. That base, of course, must be the Bible; that's
why I immerse myself in biblical materials.

So you've found your pastoral role model in Scripture?
In the process of biblical study, I found I really like being a pastor. That's my vocation: pastoral work. I discovered what God has called me to do and the gifts he has given me in order to do it. In my younger years, I often found myself doing things that were not my ministry. I finally learned to say, "No, I'm not going to do that anymore." I say no often. I disappoint many people, mostly people in the community and in my denomination. They have expectations they want me to fulfill, and I don't.

Have you also disappointed people in the congregation?
Several years ago I felt as though I were losing momentum. I quit doing many things I used to be enthusiastic about. I felt my life becoming more inward. My deepest interest is in spiritual direction, and since our community contains many psychiatrists and counselors, I quit counseling so I could spend more time alone in study and prayer. But then I found large gaps had begun to form in my congregation's life. I had underestimated the needs, and I really wasn't providing leadership. I felt my people deserved more from their pastor than they were getting. I thought maybe I belonged in a church with a staff that could be assigned tasks of parish programs, and I could study more and maintain a ministry of personal spiritual direction and of preaching.

I talked with a friend about this for three days. He listened thoughtfully and then said, "I don't think you need to leave; you just need somebody to be director of parish life." The minute he said that, I thought of Judy. She's a woman who came to me saying she was in a transitional stage, wondering where the next challenge was for her. She has organized programs for the community, done a superb job administering them, and now was relatively idle.

When I asked her if she would be director of parish life, a big grin came on her face. She said, "Let me tell you a story." Her husband was an elder, and was in the Session meeting two years earlier when I shared this problem about my leadership. After that meeting Don had come home and said, "You know what Eugene needs? He needs you." It took me two years to recognize that. And now Judy was at the place in her life where she was ready to assume this role. She needs to be in ministry and is filling some of the gap left by my withdrawal. I'm free to study more and be more sensitive to spontaneous needs within the congregation. In a sense, I had gone through a period of failure to discover grace.

Is your church growing in numbers?

Slowly. My pastoral goals are to deepen and nurture spiritual growth in people, and to build a Christian community — not collect crowds.

Could it grow faster?

Well, it could. If I did certain things we could double our membership. We could organize house-to-house visitation, advertise, bring in special speakers, create programs for the community that would tune in to some of their felt needs, or develop an entertainment-centered musical program. We could do all of those — but we'd destroy our church.

Why would that destroy it? Why don't you get 350 new people you can preach to on Sunday?

Because I'd have to quit doing what I need to do — pray, read, prepare for worship, visit, give spiritual direction to people, develop leadership in the congregation. I have to work within the limits of my abilities while I continue maturing in them.

If you speak to five thousand people and are not speaking out of your own authenticity, your own place where God has put you, you won't be any more effective as a servant of God. I don't think the number of people who hear you speak means a whole lot. What's important is that you do a good job wherever you are.

Aren't you neglecting the unchurched people of your community?

We're not the only church in Bel Air, and I'm not the only

pastor. Few places in America are unchurched. Am I going to trust the Holy Spirit to do his work through other churches in my community, or am I going to think that if we don't do it, it's not going to get done?

A great deal of arrogance develops out of the feeling that when we have something good going, we have to triple it so everybody gets in on it. Many different ministries take place in the community and in the world, and it's bad faith on my part to assume the Holy Spirit isn't just as active in them as in my ministry.

In your weekly meeting with your local ministers, what are the biggest problems you hear?

Family and marital problems. I'd say these are the most painful things in terms of pastoral crisis. Another one, which doesn't have the same sense of acuteness, is the feeling of inadequacy. When pastors don't have large congregations or don't receive affirmation from their people, it's difficult for them to provide creative spiritual leadership. In fact, considering the little affirmation many receive, I marvel that it's done at all. One of the key ministries of lay persons is affirmation of their leaders.

What counsel would you give to pastors who are in struggling situations, or who are in small churches, and are judging themselves as failures?

That's tough to answer. I'm convinced many pastors are actually doing a good job.

They don't know they are preaching and counseling and leading well. They don't expect to be perfect, but they're doing a good job.

I guess it goes back to the other themes we've talked about. A person has to be content to do what he is good at and offer it constantly to the Lord. If you keep trying to do what you're not good at, you're bound to fail. Nobody from the outside knows what the work of a pastor is, so they keep asking us to do things we're not good at, and then we end up feeling guilty for not doing a good job.

v do you get affirmation without becoming dependent on the compliments of others?

I think it has to do with discovering my need for spiritual nurture and making sure I get it. Prayer is very important for me; I can't function without it.

How does your prayer life work?

In the mornings I spend a couple of hours alone with the Lord. I get up at six o'clock and put on a pot of coffee. Often I do nothing except pray the Psalms; I've always loved them. They've been the church's prayerbook for a long time. There's an old kind of monastic nostalgia in me; in some of the monasteries all they did was pray the Psalms. I also read the New Testament, and then after an hour and a half or so I sometimes read something else or write. If I start writing, I often write for a couple of hours.

Mondays are important. For the first few years of my ministry I never took a day off. There were too many "important" things to do. Now my wife and I leave the house and go hiking in the woods for the whole day, regardless of the weather. We pack a lunch and take our binoculars for bird watching. We've been doing that every Monday for fifteen years. It's important for both of us, because it's a completely different environment and something we both enjoy doing. In the morning it's a quiet time when we can just be ourselves as well as get in touch with ourselves. At lunch we talk, and then often keep on for the rest of the afternoon.

What role has your wife played in your ministry?

A very prominent and strong one, for it's been a shared ministry. She's a marvelous entertainer, and we have people in our home often. She's a master at making people feel at home, and she's good about caring for them. She's helped create a sense of community in our church.

When we arrived, one of our goals was to develop spiritual community. I thought it would be pretty easy; we'd get these people in our home, pray together, sing some hymns, and we'd have it. Well, it didn't happen. Sometimes we felt we were making progress, but it never really happened.

Then a young woman in our congregation died of cancer. She was thirty-one years old and had six children. About a month after she died, the father was discharged from his job and then lost his house. We took those kids into our home. Suddenly things started happening. Food would appear on our doorstep; people would call up and take the kids out and entertain them. It was almost as if we came to a place of critical mass. Then it just exploded, and we suddenly had community in the congregation.

It didn't fizzle either. The hospitality increased and people took an interest in each other. It seemed almost like a miracle, and it took just one incident to trigger it. All our earlier attempts to create community now bore fruit because of the meeting of a need that wasn't part of our strategy.

I can now sense that I'm pastor of a community of people, not just a collection of neighbors.

F O U R T E E N

CARING FOR PEOPLE

The Sunday morning service is the pastor's greatest opportunity for real caring.

RICHARD C. HALVERSON

Richard C. Halverson

Dick Halverson served as pastor of Fourth Presbyterian Church in Washington, D. C., for almost twenty-three years. During that time, he built a ministry of being with people, and spent a large percentage of his breakfasts and lunches meeting with parishioners singly or in small groups.

Then, in 1981, he became chaplain of the United States Senate, where he continues his caring ministry. His activities go far beyond giving the invocation at the opening of sessions of the Senate. He offers counsel and guidance to members of Congress and their families, and countless other people on and off Capitol Hill.

A graduate of Wheaton College and Princeton Theological Seminary, Dick has written several books, been deeply involved in the prayer breakfast movement, and issued a devotional letter for leaders in business and government.

In this interview, he reflects primarily on his years as a pastoral leader and the unchanging pastoral task of caring for others.

What kind of church programs or structures foster people caring for others?

I can speak only from the viewpoint of my own ministry and experience. What works for me and the people I'm ministering with may not work for anyone else.

When I went to Fourth Presbyterian in 1958, I had come out of about twelve years of small-group ministry. I thought I was a small-group expert. I wasn't. But that's the way we operate in this culture; when you've done something for a few years, you become an expert. After my first pastorate from 1944 to 1947 at Coalinga, California, I never intended to be a pastor again, because I didn't think I was very good material. So I worked with small groups as an associate minister for nine years and then joined International Christian Leadership for about three years. After God led me to Fourth, I realized I didn't have a ready-made ministry program. In fact, I was so out of touch, I didn't even know what programs other churches were using or even what programs were available for use. I look back on that "problem" as one of the greatest assets I took to the church.

Why?

The greatest baggage a pastor carries to a new ministry, whether going from seminary to a church or changing churches, is ready-made programs. Therefore, ministries never become indigenous. It takes time to become part of what is there, to find proper adaptation and application. You can grow a dandelion in a few hours, but it takes seven years to raise an orchid.

What did you learn as you became part of Fourth?

I used to have a regular Wednesday morning breakfast with lay leaders. If I came with a burning message I had prepared in my study, invariably the guys would say to me afterward, "Halverson, it just wasn't the same this morning." It took me some time to understand there is a chemistry about each group of people that generates its own agenda. I believe it comes from the Holy Spirit in our midst. That doesn't mean I should neglect preparation, but it does mean I have to prepare with a high degree of awareness and execute with a high degree of sensitivity. When you invite a few people to your home for an evening, you don't line them up in rows and lecture them. As a small-group leader, the objective is to get them involved in the process, to get them to participate.

So in the mild frustration I experienced in those early days, God taught me two things: First, treat the Sunday morning congregation just the way you'd treat a small-group meeting in your living room. Second, implement the commandment Christ gave: "Love one another as I have loved you, and you will demonstrate to the world that you are my disciples."

But how does that small-group interaction and care happen on Sunday morning?

Even when a congregation or group is silent, something is still transmitted to the speaker. When I was a student at Princeton Seminary, Dr. Blackwood was the homiletics professor, and he used to say that 75 percent of a good sermon depends on the people.

So we'd begin every worship service with a little greeting that reminded the people of the importance of their contribution: "There is something to be captured in this moment that we can never give nor receive at any other time or in any other situation. Let's be alive to what Christ wants us to do here and now."

Then I'd try different things. I might say, "Here's what Jesus said . . . now do you hear it?" If the congregation just sat there, I'd persist, "Do we hear it?" I'd begin to get response. "What did he say?" I'd wait until somebody said it out loud from the congregation. I don't see any point in throwing words out if people are not listening and responding to them.

I believe the Sunday morning service is the pastor's greatest opportunity for real caring. For years the back page of our bulletin was called "The Family Altar" and devoted to congregational needs: the sick, shut-ins, students, four or five "Families of the Week." During our service we'd have a period of time called the "Praise and Prayers of the People." This was followed by a period of silence in which people prayed for each other. Then we asked them to touch someone near them. I'd personally step down from the pulpit and walk into the congregation and touch various people. Other pastors would do the same. Then we'd pray for the people on the back page. These simple gestures and expressions of concern create and encourage an environment of caring.

After your Sunday morning responsibilities, what did you see as your next pastoral priority?

My associates. Our weekly staff meeting was oriented toward their personal needs. Although we conducted a great deal of business in these meetings, the atmosphere was one of a family visiting together.

Next on my list of priorities was my relationship to the officers of the church. I worked at those relationships and tried to spend as much time as I could with each individual.

I was captured by a simple little statement in Mark: Jesus chose twelve and ordained them to be with him. Suddenly the word *with* became a big word, one of the biggest in the New Testament, because implicit in it is *koinonia* prayer and support. That word convinced me to have a ministry of being *with* people. I didn't worry about what I was going to do with them; I didn't need an agenda. Jesus began a movement that would be universal and last forever, and yet he spent most of his time with twelve men.

I intend my ministry to be an unstructured one — being with people at their convenience, on the job, or at breakfast or lunch. A true Christian community is not something you organize. Now I'm not saying you shouldn't have some kind of specific program, but the more spontaneous the caring is, the better.

But aren't there some specific, organized things you do?

Obviously I've long encouraged small groups, but I don't

try to organize them. It's common for people to come to me and say, "We'd like to start a small group. Will you meet with us?" I usually do, and in the first session I show them how to study the Bible inductively and encourage them to make the group experience more than just a straight Bible study. Every small group has that potential to become a support church.

Have you tried any pastoral care methodologies that didn't work?

Early on, we started the "flock system," whereby each lay leader was responsible for a certain number of members. That responsibility was clearly defined. For example, they were to meet with each member at least once a year, maintain contact at least twice a year, and so forth. It never worked. One reason was the nature of community life in metropolitan Washington. The sense of regimentation didn't seem to set very well. Some of the members said, "We don't like to be thought of as sheep." That was the final blow that killed the flock idea.

So we tried other programs. We tried fellowship committees and set up a Ministry of Concern office. If a family was being evicted or couldn't pay a hospital bill, they'd call the ministry. The ministry organized volunteers to be available to help when needed.

No program is a once-for-all solution. In all of these things we are less than perfect; we come back tomorrow and try harder.

Is home visitation effective?

When I first came to Fourth, I did a lot of conventional visitation nearly every afternoon in the week. Little by little I discovered that suburban culture doesn't allow for effective pastoral calls.

In the first place, it's almost impossible to find the family together. Second, the suburban housewife tends to be busy, and she usually doesn't see any particular value in sitting down with the pastor and visiting for thirty minutes. Third, when children are present, a pastoral call can be looked upon as family intrusion. I've had the experience of calling on families where they tried to accommodate me with one eye while watching television with the other.

In place of home visitation, we assigned each pastor the responsibility of contacting a certain number of members by phone four times a year. I'd take a couple of hours on a regular basis, sit at the phone, call a family and say, "Hi, this is Dick Halverson. I'm just calling to find out if you have any special needs I ought to be praying about today."

As a high-profile leader, how do you face the inevitable criticism that comes as a part of caring for people?

One family's fifteen-year-old boy was in trouble with the law. The father called me by telephone and leveled me about my personal failures and the failure of our church. It wasn't all true, but there was enough truth in it to make it hurt.

Even more devastating was a letter I received from one of our former elders who is now separated from his wife — two pages of nasty notes about the church's failure.

I had to face the criticism head on. In the case of the former elder, I called him. He didn't want to talk, but I persevered. I let him say everything on the telephone he had already said in the letter. Then I apologized: "I'm sorry. I'll accept this criticism for myself personally, and I'll apologize for the church." I tried to give him some explanations while bracing myself against defensiveness.

In the case of the father and son, I went first to our director of youth ministry. The night after I talked to the father, the director went to their home and spent a couple of hours talking with them.

The best way to handle criticism is to respond quickly, directly, and sensitively.

But how do you deal with the emotional trauma deep in your soul?

That's hard to answer. I suppose the most honest response would be to tell you the story about a frog who fell into a pothole. Regardless of what his frog friends tried to do, they couldn't help him out of his dilemma. Finally in desperation they left him to his destiny. The next day they found him bouncing around town as lively as ever. So one frog went up to him and said, "What happened? We thought you couldn't get out of that hole."

He replied, "I couldn't, but a truck came along and I had to."

I don't know any other answer than "you just have to." Many times I would love to run away, ignore the situation, or try to justify it, but Christ has given us specific instructions in Matthew 5:24. If you know you have offended a brother, you must go to him; if he has offended you, you must go to him. We have to do it!

In both the church and the Senate, you minister to people of all types of convictions. Yet you seem to have developed an unusual ability to love and work alongside people with whom you disagree. How have you cultivated this ability?

If I am taking my call seriously as a servant of Jesus Christ, that's my agenda, and I must be about unity, not conformity. Diversity is essential to unity. I can't imagine a painting that is all one color.

The issue is Jesus Christ, and if a person honors Christ, then that person is a brother or a sister, and we can have fellowship regardless of other differences.

Abraham Vereide, founder of what was then called International Christian Leadership, used to recite a little poem that went something like this: "He drew a circle that shut me out — heretic, rebel, a thing to flout. But love and I had the wit to win: we drew a circle that took him in."

Often the toughest place for a leader to show caring is at home. Have you found ways to overcome that?

The first element is commitment, despite the differences. I have an arrangement with Doris that God witnessed as an unconditional covenant for life. No matter how difficult it is to live together, we're going to stay married. Every struggle we have that could be used as an excuse to separate or divorce is the very material God wants us to use to create intimacy in our marriage. We can't get it any other way; it comes by hammer and heat. Good marriages are always forged.

I'll be the first to admit I've made some mistakes in my marriage and my family. During the early days of my ministry, I'd say the first eight or ten years, I equated the work of the church with God himself. I justified neglecting my wife and my children on the grounds that I was serving the Lord through the work of the church. I had to correct that. Now I believe my family is more important than the work of the church. God expects me to give priority to my wife and my children. Doris and I realize that we made some serious mistakes with our children when they were growing up. But they love us, and they are all in Christ.

I'm always amazed by the grace of God. Paul Tournier, the Swiss physician, wrote a chapter in one of his books in which he pointed out that some parents are extremely authoritarian and others are extremely permissive, but most parents are somewhere in the middle. Then he went on to say regardless of the parental style, if one's children turn out all right, it's by the grace of God. I like that — a grace that allows me to fail.

I think one of the greatest freedoms any pastor has is the freedom to fail. Again and again, in my private life and in my public ministry, I've had the pressures build until I think I can't stand it any more. When I stop long enough to take a spiritual inventory, I discover I've failed many times in the past, and it's likely that I will fail again. How liberating!

This past Tuesday morning I awakened about four o'clock after some kind of a dream about which I couldn't remember a thing except that I had failed. I tried to go back to sleep, but I couldn't relax. I finally slipped out of bed onto my knees and began to pray. As I talked to my Father, I again eventually realized that my failure does not constitute God's failure. It was so liberating to say, "Lord, when I fail, I know your grace will be there to cover the bases."

How do you deal with the many problems people bring to you?

I try to listen. It's been said many times before — which doesn't make it any less true — listening is hard work.

When I began my ministry, I had taken a required course in counseling at Princeton and had read the one or two books that were available on this subject. I wasn't well prepared to face the problems that came my way. So I had to learn counseling by listening to people. Let's face it, there is no substitute for being with people and trying to understand them and empathize with their needs.

For example, I was counseling a church member who was a closet homosexual. In our sessions I could sense he was getting close to admitting his problem. Instinctively I knew that if there was anything in my facial expression, anything at all that would indicate shock or change in attitude when he admitted his problem, I'd lose him. I so well remember how I prepared myself for the moment he shared who he was.

Have you made mistakes in counseling?

Yes, but only when I failed to spiritually prepare for my task or allowed outside pressure and personal frustrations to desensitize me to the situation.

I'm embarrassed to admit this, but early in my ministry at Fourth, a couple — she was Japanese, he was Jewish — came to me for help. Their marriage was in terrible shape; I spent hours with them. It seemed at some point in every session the young man would rise and start pacing back and forth across my office. Then he would start talking, getting louder and louder until he worked into a frenzy.

One Sunday morning they asked to see me, and he began his little act, thoroughly embarrassing and intimidating his wife. He ended his performance by saying, "If it weren't for my wife's sake, I'd take my life."

By then I was fed up with him, and in anger I said, "Well, you sure aren't much use to her now."

Monday morning I found he had attempted to take his life. I

went to the hospital, and the first thing he said was, "Mr. Halverson, you told me to do it."

I had failed him — both of them — because I stopped listening and allowed myself to become insensitive to the real problem. Even to this day I rarely give what might be considered direct advice.

Some pastors might find it difficult to identify with your warm, vulnerable personality. How do they develop a caring ministry?

I think of Louis Evans, Jr., pastor of National Presbyterian Church. All of the vocational and aptitude tests he took disqualified him for the pastorate. Louis thinks mechanically. He's orderly. The tests say he should be an engineer. He'd rather take an engine apart and put it together again than almost anything in the world. But God called him to be a pastor, and he persevered in spite of the tests and has developed a tremendous ministry.

Some of the most successful pastors I know have been poor preachers but tremendous with people. Others have been poor with people and tremendous in the pulpit. If God is calling you to be a pastor, he's going to put you in a ministry situation that needs your skills. A person cannot foreclose on God's plans because of self-perceived weaknesses. It usually doesn't occur to us that we might not have liked the apostle Paul. Several Scripture passages indicate he might have been an abrasive person, and everyone agrees that Peter was a hard person to get along with.

How would you describe Dick Halverson?

In some ways I'm a very private person. I've always struggled with low self-image. Because of that image I'm easily intimidated. To this day, if I have to walk into a room of strangers, I must brace myself for the experience. Although I think I have accepted my low self-image, I compensate for it with a gregarious air. But if I'm not careful, I find myself resenting the intrusions of people into my life. Thus, I must keep working with myself; for in my own eyes, a pastor or chaplain must be a people person, a servant of the servants of the Servant.

What process did you go through to move your self-image from the liability to the asset column?
Part of it goes back to the origins of my low self-image. Mother married my father against the will of her parents. My father was an itinerant worker. He'd ride railroad freight cars to the Midwest where he worked as a harvest laborer. Then he would return to his home in St. Paul and live on his wages. He was a kind person, soft-spoken, gentle, a good dancer, and handsome; but my mother soon discovered he was irresponsible. He never did support the family. When I was ten years old my parents divorced — in a little North Dakota town where nobody got divorced — and we moved into a flat where we shared a bathroom with twenty families. I can still hear the cockroaches crush in the doorjamb when I closed the door.

I've been afraid of my father's traits all of my life. To this day, I feel there is something in me that wants to run as far away from responsibility as I can get.

As a youth I compensated for my circumstances with arrogance. Apparently I was born with a gift for singing, for people seemed to enjoy my efforts at entertainment and encouraged me to seek a career in the theater. That became my burning ambition until I met the Lord at twenty years of age, and he made it clear that he had another plan for my life.

How did the Lord make that plan clear to you?
A pastor began to deal with me. He helped me see my arrogance — that there was no substance to it, and that I was covering up those awful fears I had about my inadequacy.

He showed me how to study the Scriptures. The verse that helped me turn the corner was Paul's marvelous testimony that in weakness he became strong. In 2 Corinthians 12 he says, "Lest I be exalted above measure, a thorn in the flesh was given to me." And in another incredible passage, 1 Corinthians 15, he says, "Last of all, Christ appeared to me also as one born out of due time and not worthy to be called an apostle because I persecuted the church of God. Nevertheless, by the grace of God, I am what I am."

I grabbed that truth with both hands as my valid place of self-acceptance; by the grace of God, I am what I am.

How do you keep this spiritual truth at the heart of your ministry in a highly visible setting?

During the nine years I ministered in Hollywood, California, I observed that the one thing that destroyed more prominent people than anything else was the temptation to believe in their own publicity.

Do you recall the Old Testament story in which three of David's soldiers overheard him say, "Oh, if I could only have some water from the well in Jerusalem"? At the risk of their lives, they sneaked through the enemy lines to bring him a drink of water.

But he refused to drink it; he knew they had risked their lives for it. So he poured it out as a libation to God.

That has become a symbol for me when I receive any praise or credit. I'm thankful for it. I know I have an ego that loves to hear it, but I refuse to accept it. I pour it out to Christ.